100 THINGS
OKLAHOMA FANS
SHOULD KNOW & DO
BEFORE THEY DIE

100 THINGS
OKLAHOMA FANS
SHOULD KNOW & DO
BEFORE THEY DIE

Steve Richardson

TRIUMPH
B O O K S

The Library of Congress has catalogued the previous edition as follows:

Richardson, Steve.
  100 things Oklahoma fans should know and do before they die / Steve Richardson.
   p. cm.
   ISBN 978-1-60078-272-5
    1. Oklahoma Sooners (Football team)—History. 2. University of Oklahoma—Football—History. I. Title. II. Title: One hundred things Oklahoma fans should know and do before they die.
   GV958.O4R53 2009
   796.332'6300766—dc22

                                                              2009007265

This book is available in quantity at special discounts for your group or organization. For further information, contact:
   Triumph Books LLC
   814 North Franklin Street
   Chicago, Illinois 60610
   (312) 337-0747
   www.triumphbooks.com

Printed in U.S.A.
ISBN: 978-1-62937-007-1
Design by Patricia Frey
Photos courtesy of AP Images unless otherwise indicated

To all the past presidents of the Football Writers Association of America and to Volney Meece

Contents

Acknowledgments

Putting together a book of this nature requires a full under-standing of the University of Oklahoma football culture. Since covering and watching Oklahoma football games and the Big 8 (now Big 12) Conference since the 1970s, I have run into a number of people with OU ties as well as key figures in the Sooners family. They have been invaluable in helping develop information for this book.

Over the years Barry Switzer, Dean Blevins, Joe Castiglione, Bob Stoops, Kenny Mossman, the late Lee Roy Selmon, the late Prentice Gautt, and many, many writers such as Dave Sittler, George Schroeder, Berry Tramel, and John Rohde have helped with their great insight into the Sooners.

Special thanks go to J.D. Roberts and Tommy McDonald for providing this writer a glimpse into the Bud Wilkinson era; De De Jarman, a long-time Sooners wife who had married a favorite player under Wilkinson; Donnie Duncan, who was an OU assistant football coach in the 1970s and later the athletics director at OU; former Orange Bowl Executive Director and Big 8 Associate Commissioner Steve Hatchell, a football manager for Eddie Crowder and who worked with Gautt; Bill Hancock, who worked for Harold Keith and with Gautt; John Underwood, a former associate athletics director at OU; Frank Wolfson, an OU letter-winner; and Jim Dickey, a former OU assistant coach and later head coach at Kansas State.

Further thanks go to Errol McKoy, president of the State Fair of Texas; Bob Sambol, former owner of Bob's Steak & Chop House; Lynne Draper, former executive director of the Jim Thorpe Association; and Gil Brandt, one-time vice-president of player personnel for the Dallas Cowboys. Over the years, former

Longhorns coach and player David McWilliams has always provided a Texas slant to the OU series.

All have helped greatly. And I hope they, as well as readers, enjoy the book.

Introduction

The Oklahoma Sooners are considered one of the storied programs in college football history. Since World War II, Oklahoma has led the nation with 598 victories going into the 2014 season.

There's little doubt why: seven national championships, five Heisman Trophy winners, a couple dozen College Football Hall of Fame coaches and players, and the longest winning streak in major college football history. The Sooners have produced All-Americans on an assembly line and have won conference championships with regularity—41 times since the mid-1930s.

Because some very good players and teams became merely footnotes, this book is packed full of interesting sidebars in order to accommodate them.

Oklahoma football's first big-name coach, Bennie Owen, from 1905 to 1926, started a tradition of exciting offensive football that has existed in Norman for more than a century. Owen produced four unbeaten teams and helped lead a campaign to finance the bonds to build Memorial Stadium in the mid-1920s. Then in 1938 Tom Stidham coached the Sooners to the Orange Bowl—their first of 47 bowl appearances through the 2013 season.

The hit Broadway musical *Oklahoma!* in the 1940s ushered in a tradition of Oklahoma football that, associated with the popularity of New York Yankees stars and Oklahoma natives Mickey Mantle and Allie Reynolds, became a magical time for Oklahomans in the 1950s. And No. 47 became popular because of the OU football winning streak from 1953 to 1957.

Oklahoma football in the modern era can be grouped into three great periods by coaches: Bud Wilkinson (1947–1963), Barry Switzer (1973–1988), and Bob Stoops (1999–present). All the national title teams and four of the five Heisman Trophy winners have played during those eras. Still, the 1971 team of coach Chuck

Fairbanks with star runner Greg Pruitt was possibly the best team in college football history to fail to win the national title.

While coaches like Wilkinson, Switzer, and Stoops have grabbed headlines, several great Sooners players have contributed greatly to the success of the program over the years. Besides the Heisman Trophy winners, Oklahoma has had multiple winners of the Outland Trophy (five), Butkus Award (four), Lombardi Trophy (three), Davey O'Brien Award (three), Thorpe Award (three), Maxwell Award (two), Nagurski Trophy (two), and Walter Camp Award (four). That's not to mention the hundreds of All-Conference players at the school.

Buzzwords associated with Oklahoma football also give this book flavor. Nicknames and places such as "the Boz," "O'Connell's," "Little Joe," "the Tunnel," and "the Kick" are forever etched in Sooners lore and must be remembered. The great games against Nebraska in the old Big 8 Conference produced some of the Sooners' greatest comebacks—known as "Sooner Magic."

Having watched most of the Oklahoma-Texas games in person since the mid-1980s at the Cotton Bowl in Dallas, I know there is no better regular-season setting in college football. Some of those moments and images are included in the following pages.

Today, after decades of excellence, the popularity of Oklahoma football is at an all-time high. That's why this is the perfect time to catalog the 100 things Oklahoma fans should know and do before they die.

1 Bud Wilkinson

The true Sooners tradition began with Bud Wilkinson in 1947. He laid the foundation for perhaps the greatest dynasty in college football history, from the late 1940s to the late 1950s, and created the Midland saying "Oklahoma and the Seven Dwarfs" in reference to OU's supremacy over its conference.

Such had been OU's domination of first the Big 7, from 1948 to 1957, and then the Big 8 Conference that the Sooners went from 1947—Wilkinson's first season as OU's head coach—until 1959 without losing a league game.

One of the reasons Frank Broyles left Missouri for Arkansas after coaching in Columbia, Missouri, for just the 1957 season was the fact he saw little hope other teams in the league could compete with the juggernaut in Norman. While this ultimately proved not to be the case, when OU began to decline in the early 1960s under Wilkinson as Missouri and Nebraska flourished, Broyles' initial fears certainly were not unfounded. Missouri, as an example, went from 1946 until 1960 without beating the Sooners.

Wilkinson's program was astonishingly consistent and well-detailed. And his players served him with unquestioned loyalty. In Oklahoma he was king, having delivered the state from the throes of the Depression and Dust Bowl and into post–World War II football heaven. One wife of an early 1960s OU football player remarked years later, "When Bud walked into a room, everybody just stopped. He was the king."

"You never questioned Wilkinson," said OU's star halfback of the mid-1950s, Tommy McDonald. "He was so big. You never

Bud Wilkinson poses with his 1949 Coach of the Year plaque at a dinner sponsored by the American Football Coaches Association in New York on January 12, 1950.

thought about questioning Bud Wilkinson. You would never put that in your mind at all. What Bud said, that was it."

Wearing a gray suit, a tie, and a fedora, Wilkinson was the forerunner of the Dallas Cowboys' Tom Landry sideline look. And the former quarterback and guard modeled himself after his college coach, Bernie Bierman of Minnesota, in the early 1930s.

"He was the most organized coach I ever worked for," said OU's 1953 Outland Trophy winner J.D. Roberts, who was a Wilkinson assistant coach, then an assistant for several other prominent coaches at other schools, and finally head coach of the New Orleans Saints. "Our practices were totally organized, there would be so much time for this, and that, and on down the line.

"I remember during this one meeting he said, 'Football is complicated and it is always easy to omit something in planning.' So he wanted really everyone to think ahead and be prepared and make sure we didn't omit something we needed to get done."

Wilkinson's OU teams claimed three national titles, won six of eight bowl games, and finished first in the conference every year from 1946 to 1959. His teams produced a 47-game winning streak—the longest in college football history—from 1953 to 1957. While what he said was gospel, he rarely had to raise his voice to inspire his players.

"These guys didn't just adore Bud, Bud was their life," said Steve Hatchell, one-time team manager and scout team scrub for Colorado coach Eddie Crowder, Wilkinson's former player at OU. "And so when those guys started to talk about what it meant to be part of that system, [it was something]. I haven't been around every football program in the country. But there's nothing compared to what it meant to that state. It wasn't a state until 1907.... Everybody looked down on it. It was nothing but a truck stop."

During his final four seasons (1960 through 1963), Oklahoma won only one Big 8 title, in 1962, and Wilkinson failed to beat Texas the last six times he played the Longhorns. He retired from college coaching after the 1963 season, then failed in his 1964 bid for a U.S. Senate seat. He went into sports commentating for ABC and did many of the big games of the era, including the 1971 Game of the Century between Oklahoma and Nebraska.

Inducted into the College Football Hall of Fame in 1969, Wilkinson later became coach of the St. Louis Football Cardinals in 1978, but lasted less than two seasons and returned to broadcasting. He passed away in 1994 at the age of 77.

2 Barry Switzer

The Barry Switzer coaching era in Norman was separated by a decade and three coaches from Bud Wilkinson's button-down regime. Wilkinson and Switzer were light years apart in their approach to the game and personal temperament.

Despite their different approaches to coaching, Switzer would produce three national title teams (1974, 1975, and 1985), just as Wilkinson did (1950, 1955, and 1956). And their overall records at the school were quite similar—Switzer was 157–29–4 in 16 seasons, and Wilkinson was 145–29–4 in 17.

Wilkinson's father owned a mortgage company. He attended military school before he played guard and quarterback for Bernie Bierman's national championship teams at Minnesota from 1934 to 1936. He even wanted to be an English teacher at one time. Switzer had a poor and sometimes tragic family background in Arkansas, as related in his book *Bootlegger's Boy*. He played under Coach Frank Broyles at Arkansas as a center and linebacker and was captain of the 1959 team that won the Southwest Conference and beat Georgia Tech in the Gator Bowl.

"He hugged all the kids," said Donnie Duncan, an assistant coach at OU from 1973 to 1978 and later Switzer's athletics director. "He loved them. I was recruiting a kid over in Greenville, Texas—Richard Murray. He was raised by a momma and two aunts. His father had been killed in an automobile accident. His mother's name was Irene. We go to the [Murray] home. Switzer picked her up and started swinging her around, and she said, 'Coach Switzer, put me down!' He was saying, 'Good night, Irene. Good night, Irene.'"

Wilkinson could have coached ballet with his etiquette on the sideline. Switzer was often impromptu and theatrical in his gestures and actions—he would call recruits at halftime, scream at officials, and allow his players to lounge on the sideline in routs of the Big 8's downtrodden. But he always seemed to know just what to say to inspire great players to even greater heights.

"I think it was what defined him," said Dean Blevins, an OU quarterback in the mid-1970s. "While he is better at Xs and Os and coached better than most people realize, there was a magic about him. He was motivational.... He was positive. He would say, 'We have got little Joe [Washington]. He will have a big game today.... You, 'Little Joe,' are going to dazzle them. Go out and get 150. Steve [Davis], get the ball out to Tinker [Owens]. Nebraska is not going to move the ball on you, Rod Shoate. Nobody is going to move the ball on you, Randy Hughes.'"

It all seemed to work during the free-wheeling 1970s and later in the 1980s. After the Sooners installed the wishbone in the early 1970s, when Chuck Fairbanks was still the head coach, Switzer took it and ran the Sooners into national prominence once again. Bootlegger's Boy recruited well and understood an entire new generation and ethnicity of players. Barry had style. And the wishbone was stylish. And his players had style.

"One, I think he understood African American kids," said Steve Hatchell, who was an associate commissioner in the Big 8

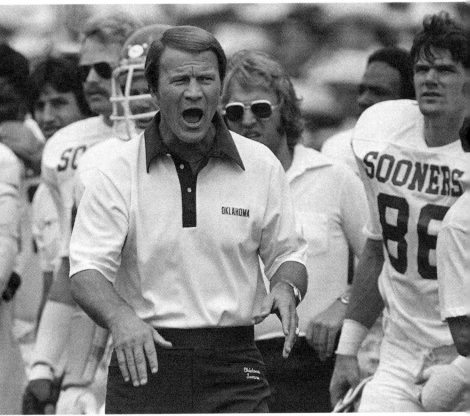

Barry Switzer screams instructions from the sideline during a game against Texas in the Cotton Bowl on October 10, 1981.

Conference office from 1977 to 1983 and later was the Orange Bowl's executive director. "And I think he just understood kids to begin with, whether they were black or white, what they wanted to do, how they wanted to play. Jimmy Johnson was a little bit of the same way—he knew when to turn on the pressure and when not to. It was emblematic of a change from the heavily regimented looks to a Switzer-type of thing."

Switzer's teams won or shared 12 Big 8 Conference championships and competed in 10 New Year's Day bowl games, including nine Orange Bowls. His 16 teams had 109 All–Big 8 Conference selections and a galaxy of stars, including Heisman Trophy winner running back Billy Sims (1978), Outland Trophy winner defensive tackle Lee Roy Selmon (1975), two-time Butkus Award winner linebacker Brian Bosworth (1984 and 1985), and Lombardi Trophy winner nose guard Tony Casillas (1985).

The 16-year run at Oklahoma ended for Switzer, who resigned in June 1989 after three serious law-breaking off-the-field incidents involving five Sooners football players. The program was also serving a three-year NCAA probation at the time of his resignation. But Switzer eventually wound up as coach of the Dallas Cowboys in 1994 and a year later coached them to a Super Bowl title. Switzer was inducted into the College Football Hall of Fame in 2001.

47 Straight

Like Joe DiMaggio's unmatched 56-game major-league hitting streak, Oklahoma's 47-game winning streak in college football is almost mythical in its enduring nature. It has been 57 years since it ended in 1957, and no college team has really come close to matching it.

The closest have been 1) USC winning 34 straight from 2003 to 2005, and finally losing to Texas 41–38 in the 2006 Rose Bowl; and 2) Miami (Fla.) also matching that figure from 2000 to 2002, ending in a controversial 31–24 double overtime loss to Ohio State in the 2003 Fiesta Bowl. But those clubs were still 13 victories short of even tying Bud Wilkinson's squad's streak.

Wilkinson's 1953 team opened the season with a 28–21 home loss to Notre Dame and a 7–7 tie at Pittsburgh.

The 47 Straight Victories

1953 (9–1–1)

Notre Dame	L	28–21
at Pitt	T	7–7
Texas*	W	19–14
Kansas	W	45–0
Colorado	W	27–20
Kansas State	W	34–0
at Missouri	W	14–0
Iowa State	W	47–0
at Nebraska	W	30–7
Oklahoma State	W	42–7
Maryland	W	7–0 (Orange Bowl)

1954 (10–0)

at California	W	27–13
TCU	W	21–16
Texas*	W	14–7
at Kansas	W	65–0
Kansas State	W	21–0
at Colorado	W	13–6
at Iowa State	W	40–0
Missouri	W	34–13
Nebraska	W	55–7
at Oklahoma State	W	14–0

1955 (11–0)

at North Carolina	W	13–6
Pittsburgh	W	26–14
Texas*	W	20–0
Kansas	W	44–6
Colorado	W	56–21
at Kansas State	W	40–7
at Missouri	W	20–0
Iowa State	W	52–0
at Nebraska	W	41–0
Oklahoma State	W	53–0
Maryland	W	20–6 (Orange Bowl)

1956 (10–0)

North Carolina	W	36–0
Kansas State	W	66–0
Texas*	W	45–0
at Kansas	W	34–12
at Notre Dame	W	40–0
at Colorado	W	27–19
at Iowa State	W	44–0
Missouri	W	67–14
Nebraska	W	54–6
at Oklahoma State	W	53–0

1957 (10–1)

at Pittsburgh	W	26–0
Iowa State	W	40–14
Texas*	W	21–7
Kansas	W	47–0
Colorado	W	14–13
At Kansas State	W	13–0
At Missouri	W	39–14
Notre Dame	*L*	*7–0*
at Nebraska	W	32–7
Oklahoma State	W	53–6
Duke	W	48–21 (Orange Bowl)

All Texas games were played at the Cotton Bowl in Dallas

"Against Notre Dame, we had a lot of sophomores playing," said former OU lineman J.D. Roberts, who won the Outland Trophy that season as a senior. "We actually played fairly well.… It was a day game, very hot…we held them to less yards rushing than they had against anyone else all year…we had a chance to tie it at the end and we dropped a pass. We moved the ball pretty well."

But at Pittsburgh, the offense was bogged down. There was no reason to believe the next week, against Texas, a 47-game winning streak would begin.

"We did know one thing," Roberts said. "We had a damn good freshman class.... We would scrimmage them some, and they had some fine football players…Jerry Tubbs, Jimmy Harris, Tommy McDonald."

Without those freshmen (who were not eligible to play) in 1953, the streak started with a 19–14 victory over the Longhorns when OU jumped out to a 19–0 lead. The Sooners' Merrill Green returned a punt 80 yards for a touchdown, and Oklahoma withstood two late Texas scores. The Longhorns couldn't overcome five fumbles. OU shut out five opponents the rest of the 1953 season and upset already-crowned national champion Maryland 7–0 in the Orange Bowl.

In 1954 halfback McDonald, linebacker-center-fullback Tubbs, and quarterback Jimmy Harris took over and posted a 31–0 record during their three seasons. Oklahoma finished 10–0 in 1954 but behind No. 1 Ohio State and No.2 UCLA in both major polls. The Sooners won back-to-back national titles in 1955 (11–0) and 1956 (10–0). And while these were well-oiled offensive machines, the Sooners shut out 11 of 21 opponents over those 1955 and 1956 seasons.

Even with Harris, McDonald, and Tubbs gone, Oklahoma was still formidable. The Sooners won their first seven games of the 1957 season before playing host to Notre Dame on November 16 in Norman. Second-ranked Oklahoma had scored in 123-straight contests, was averaging 300 yards rushing a game, and was favored by nearly three touchdowns.

Oklahoma moved down to the Irish 13 on its first possession, was thwarted, and never got any closer to scoring for the rest of the game. The Sooners managed just 98 yards rushing, and OU coach Bud Wilkinson said he was prepared to accept a 0–0 tie when the Sooners couldn't get anything going in the third period. In the fourth quarter Notre Dame went on a 20-play, 80-yard drive and scored on a fourth-down, three-yard run by Dick Lynch on a pitch from quarterback Bob Williams with 3:50 left.

Williams intercepted an OU pass in the end zone with less than a minute to go to wrap up the victory for Notre Dame, which had lost to OU 40–0 the previous season in South Bend.

"We prepared for them in detail," said Fighting Irish coach Terry Brennan after he had been carried off the field on a couple of his players' shoulders. "We didn't have a whole lot of speed, and we tried to be as basic as possible. There were only four or five basic plays [for Oklahoma's offense]—and if you stopped them, you had a chance to win. The big thing was to stop their running game."

Fans cried in the stands. Many in attendance rose in appreciation to give the Sooners a standing ovation at the game's end. Many just stayed in their seats in stunned disbelief long after the game. "It's just like death," said OU tackle Doyle Jennings. "But after it has happened, there is nothing you can do about it, so you might as well forget it."

McDonald, with the Philadelphia Eagles in 1957, gave his reaction when he found out about the end of the streak: "Stunned. I can imagine what he [Wilkinson] might have said, 'Now, do you see what you have done to yourselves? You have done it, are you happy?'"

4 1956 National Title Team

Entering the 1956 season, the Sooners were riding a 30-game winning streak and holding the No. 1 ranking in college football. And this perhaps was the most dominating season in Oklahoma football history. Oklahoma dropped out of the No. 1 spot twice during the regular season but regained the top spot late in the season and held off all challengers.

The 1956 campaign, with halfback Tommy McDonald and center Jerry Tubbs returning for their senior seasons, got off to a rousing start with a 36–0 walloping of North Carolina in Norman. The Sooners had managed only a seven-point victory over the Tar Heels the previous season. Wilkinson's best team followed that up with shut outs of Kansas State (66–0) and bitter rival Texas (45–0). That Longhorns loss was UT coach Ed Price's final appearance at the Cotton Bowl.

As good an offensive team as the 1955 OU squad was, the 1956 team was even better. Once again, Oklahoma led the nation in total offense (481.7 yards a game), 71 yards better than 1955. Once again, the Sooners were the best rushing team in the land (391 yards a game), more than 62 yards better than the previous season. And once again, OU topped the country in scoring (46.6 ppg), about 10 more points a game than in 1955. End Ed Bell, back Clendon Thomas, tackles Ed Gray and Tom Emerson, and guard Bill Krisher were other stars of that team.

Oklahoma played only four games in Norman that season. The Sooners actually went on an extended road trip after October 6 until returning November 17 to Norman, but won games at the neutral site in Dallas against Texas, and at Kansas, Notre Dame, Colorado, and Iowa State. After the Notre Dame game, the remaining teams on the schedule knew that what Notre Dame quarterback Paul Hornung told reporters after the game was probably true, that Oklahoma wasn't that big, "but they were always there."

The 40–0 victory in South Bend was particularly notable because it was dominating and on the road over a team that had the fair-haired Hornung, who would win the Heisman Trophy that season despite Notre Dame posting a losing record. Maybe they divided up the Oklahoma vote, but McDonald and Tubbs would finish third and fourth, respectively, in the 1956 Heisman Trophy voting behind Hornung and Tennessee halfback Johnny Majors.

What happened the next week at Colorado was inexplicable. The Buffaloes, in their mile-high altitude, took a 19–6 halftime lead. Colorado slashed OU's defense for touchdowns on two long drives and blocked an OU quick kick for another score. Wilkinson's speech at halftime of that game is one McDonald can distinctly remember more than 50 years later.

"We got in there at halftime, and Bud Wilkinson said, 'Take those jerseys off. You don't deserve to wear those jerseys. That jersey has a reputation of winning!'" McDonald said. "The one good thing about Wilkinson, he was a super, super motivational talker."

Things turned around for the Sooners thereafter. Wilkinson's message got through to his undefeated team, which was riding a 35-game winning streak going into the game and rallied for a 27–19 victory. The Sooners followed with lopsided victories over Iowa State, Missouri, Nebraska, and Oklahoma State by a combined score of 218–20.

For the second time in four years, Oklahoma had an unbeaten team that couldn't go to the Orange Bowl because of the Big 7's no-repeat edict, which would be lifted later in the decade, allowing OU to go to back-to-back bowls in Miami. So the Sooners' 1956 season ended after the Oklahoma State victory. The senior class of which Tubbs and McDonald were a part finished a remarkable 31–0 in varsity competition—truly a golden era in Sooners football.

"I didn't even realize [that we hadn't lost a game] until my senior year, when everybody said we had to win these games and we could go through college without ever losing a game," McDonald said.

5 Bob Stoops

Bob Stoops comes from deep in Midwestern football territory, with a coaching pedigree that was developed under a lineage of standout coaches.

Ohio born and bred, Stoops grew up in Youngstown and played high school football at Cardinal Mooney. He was a four-year starter as an Iowa defensive back in the late 1970s and early 1980s. He stayed in Iowa City and coached for Hayden Fry for five years. After a year at Kent State, he then moved to Kansas State as an assistant under Bill Snyder for seven years, first coaching the defensive backs and then becoming co–defensive coordinator.

When he was defensive coordinator at Florida from 1996 to 1998, he matched wits with offensive-minded head coach Steve Spurrier, causing one former Florida official to reminisce about their great game strategy chess matches in practice. To this day, Spurrier and Stoops remain close. Spurrier calls Bob "Stoopsey."

"You take something from everybody," Stoops said on the eve of playing in his fourth national title game in early 2009, this time against Florida. "Coach Fry, I thought he was a great leader and did a great job with his assistant coaches. Coach Snyder was a very determined guy and was at the ground floor at Kansas State, and I learned a lot from that experience. Coach Spurrier was just an amazing competitor, and I felt I learned to really love the competition of it all from watching him, being around him."

In 1998 OU athletics director Joe Castiglione made perhaps the most important Sooners football hire of the 20th century when he selected an *assistant coach*, Stoops, to lead the Sooner nation out of the football wilderness.

Bob Stoops addresses the crowd at the Sooners' championship celebration program in Norman on January 21, 2001, where he told the audience estimated at 30,000 that he wants to be head football coach for years to come. Oklahoma capped its 13–0 season with a 13–2 victory over Florida State in the Orange Bowl on January 3.

In the previous nine seasons, from 1990 to 1998, before Stoops arrived, Oklahoma had a losing conference record (31–33–2) and was only 5–29–2 against ranked teams. The Sooners had not won a league title since 1987, in Barry Switzer's next-to-last season at the school. The Sooners had gone four seasons without a bowl bid or a winning record. That quickly changed. Stoops took the Sooners to the Independence Bowl his first season in 1999 and then won a national championship in 2000, the school's seventh and first since 1985.

The Sooners were back.

In Stoops' first 15 seasons in Norman, the Sooners won or shared eight Big 12 Conference titles. On November 23, 2013, he passed Switzer as the winningest coach in OU history when the Sooners defeated Kansas State 41–31 in Manhattan. Under Stoops, Oklahoma has finished in the Associated Press final top 25 in all but two seasons, and nine of those times the team has wound up in the top 10.

Stoops ranks tied for third among major-college coaches in longevity at their current schools behind only Virginia Tech's Frank Beamer and Troy's Larry Blakeney entering the 2014 season. He also has averaged more victories per season (10.7) than any coach in major-college football who has coached at least 10 seasons.

"In the end, I am just proud of our program, overall, and what we have been able to do…. and when you compare it to what was happening the 10 years prior," Stoops said. "It isn't just me. It's a great administration. It's a bunch of great assistant coaches who we have had here, and good character and players that have helped build and get the program back in a strong position."

6 Billy Vessels

Go to Heisman Park near Gaylord Family–Oklahoma Memorial Stadium and see the statue of Billy Vessels. The Sooners' first Heisman Trophy winner, in 1952, was born in Cleveland, Oklahoma, during the Great Depression. And before he arrived at the University of Oklahoma in the late 1940s, he led a hardscrabble life in what was a state swept by first the Dust Bowl and then World War II.

By the mid-1940s, Vessels was on his own when his family moved to Oklahoma City. Years later he told friends the town of Cleveland basically supported him when he stayed with different families and did odd jobs to help support himself.

Finally, Robert H. Breeden, a publisher of the *Cleveland American* newspaper, befriended Vessels and introduced him to Oklahoma Sooners football games. And when Oklahoma coach Bud Wilkinson saw what a good player he was, Vessels agreed to come to OU and play football.

"When he was in high school, he was told that he was a terrific football player, but you are never going to make it at Oklahoma," said National Football Foundation executive director Steve Hatchell, who became a friend of Vessels years later. "He was told you are not going to get into college unless you start reading books.

"Billy Vessels later talked a lot about Bud's influence on all of their lives. When you learned about how hardscrabble his life had been, where he was from in Oklahoma—you want to talk about down and out, he came from the poorest of circumstances and his high school couldn't have gotten him educated if they had wanted to—there was no way he was going to make it at Oklahoma.

"Later on, I heard Billy talk about that. People who go to college read books. They understand what is there. They can give you a test. You have to learn. You have to learn what is out there. You better learn to read."

Vessels, nicknamed "Curly," learned to read, was tutored by well-meaning friends, went to college, and eventually won the Heisman Trophy as a senior in 1952.

"Vessels was the best back we ever have had there, quite frankly," said OU's 1953 Outland Trophy winner J.D. Roberts. "He wasn't only an offensive back. He was a hell of a defensive back. And he played some on defense early on."

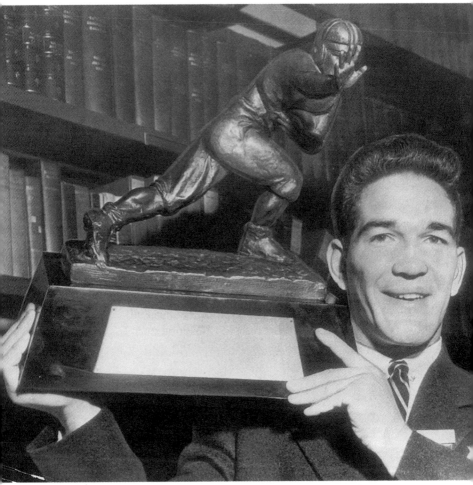

Billy Vessels holds his 1952 Heisman Trophy. Vessels was an All-American in 1952 and was the first Oklahoma player to win the Heisman. In 1950 he led Oklahoma in rushing and receiving and helped lead the Sooners to their first national title.

As a sophomore at OU, the 6', 185-pound Vessels broke upon the national scene in the third game of the 1950 season against archrival Texas. Vessels scored a touchdown late in the fourth quarter to tie the score 13–13. The extra point gave OU a 14–13 victory. Vessels also had scored OU's earlier touchdown in the game.

He not only kept OU's 24-game winning streak intact, he helped propel the Sooners to their first national title that year with 938 yards rushing (6.1 yards a carry) and 13 rushing touchdowns. He also caught 13 passes for 250 yards and a couple of scores.

In 1951 Vessels was part of a backfield that included Eddie Crowder, Buck McPhail, and Frank Silva. But he suffered a knee injury early in the season in a 9–7 loss to Texas and finished with only 27 rushing attempts.

"It was on a 28-option play," Roberts said. "It was a pitch back to him, and it was either a bad pitch or he missed the pitch or something, and he went back, and one of their ends hit him. He got his knee tore up and he was lost for the season. He really got to play only two full games in his junior year."

Vessels rehabbed during the offseason by running barefoot in the sandy shore along the Arkansas River near his hometown. With his knee back in shape in 1952, he came back and became the Sooners' first 1,000-yard rusher in a season. Oklahoma finished the season 8–1–1. Despite a 27–21 loss at Notre Dame, Vessels still gained 195 yards and scored three touchdowns against the Fighting Irish in Oklahoma's first national television appearance. That went a long way to Vessels' winning the Heisman Trophy. "That Vessels boy is one of the best runners we've ever seen," Notre Dame coach Frank Leahy said.

Vessels played one season in Canada for the Edmonton Eskimos and was the MVP of what became the forerunner of the Canadian Football League. He had a brief stint in the U.S. Army and then played one season in the NFL with the Baltimore Colts, the team that drafted him out of Oklahoma. Vessels went into private business in Florida and later served on the Florida State Racing Commission. He was inducted into the College Football Hall of Fame in 1974 and passed away in 2001 at the age of 70.

7 The Selmons

Oklahoma's 1975 Outland and Lombardi Trophy winner Lee Roy Selmon passed away in 2011, but the chain of restaurants on the west coast of Florida lives on, with several in the St. Petersburg/ Tampa area. Selmon's restaurants feature many of the recipes and food his mother used to serve him and his brothers on the farm back in Oklahoma. The restaurants also have a bar area for watching sporting events on flat-screen TVs and plenty of memorabilia from Selmon's playing days as a Sooner and a Tampa Bay Buccaneer.

"Opening our restaurants here in the Tampa Bay area has been a very exciting time for me and my family," Selmon said several years ago. "It is rewarding to see our customers enjoying the cooking traditions I remember from the days spent on our farm in Oklahoma, where our family learned to harvest the land together. That was where our parents planted the seeds of love, faith, and hard work that remain in our lives today."

Some of the restaurant's specialties include fried green tomatoes, Mama's meatloaf, Selmon's sweet heat fried chicken, and cheese and bacon grits. Other favorites are smokin' ribs (pork and chicken with a choice of four homemade sauces), "two-handed" burgers and sandwiches, smoked chicken salad, and citrus glazed shrimp salad. And don't forget the deserts, such as Georgia peach cobbler, pecan pie, and the signature "Selmon's Super Sunday Crunch."

Selmon, a 6'3", 256-pound defensive tackle, was voted as the top Sooner in history by the *Daily Oklahoman* in its 2007 state centennial ratings of the 100 best football players at the school. Coach Barry Switzer said flatly that Selmon is the best player he ever

One of Mama Selmon's Favorite Recipes for a Tailgate

Smokey Bacon Cheese Dip*
6–8 slices of applewood smoked bacon, cooked crisp
8 oz. sour cream
8 oz. bleu cheese
6 oz. cream cheese, softened
1/4 c. minced onion
hot sauce to taste
2 Tbsp. of snipped fresh chives

Cook bacon until crisp, drain on towel, cool. Set aside. Place remaining ingredients in bowl of food processor fitted with blade. Crumble bacon over top of mixture. Process until combined. The recipe can be made up to 24 hours before the game. Serve with crackers, chips, and/or sliced vegetables.

*From Lee Roy Selmon's Restaurant website

coached. He also was one of the smartest, being named a National Football Foundation Scholar Athlete as a senior.

The first overall player taken in the 1976 NFL Draft by the expansion Tampa Bay Buccaneers, Selmon played for Tampa Bay from 1976 to 1984 and was named to six straight Pro Bowls. He was inducted into the College Football Hall of Fame in 1988 and the Pro Football Hall of Fame in 1995. He was one of three Selmon brothers who played at OU.

Quite possibly, the Selmon brothers—Lucious, Dewey, and Lee Roy—are the most famous trio of brothers to ever play defense for a college football team at one time. Hailing from Eufaula, Oklahoma, a farming community of 2,500 people about 125 miles east of Norman, the trio grew up doing farm chores instead of lifting weights.

They lived in a four-room house on 40 acres of farmland. The house didn't have running water or an indoor bathroom. Water came from a well, and cooking was done on a wood stove. The three football-playing sons were the youngest of the family of nine children raised by Lucious Sr. and Jessie Selmon.

But there was a recipe for success: the brothers helped their father farm with a mule-team (strength and conditioning), they often ate what they raised in the fields (nutrition), and their family playbook was the Bible (morals and character).

Lucious Selmon (No. 98) was two years ahead of his brothers, Lee Roy (No. 93) and Dewey (91), and played at OU as a sophomore in 1971 when the Sooners lost the Game of the Century to Nebraska 35–31. The other two Selmons didn't arrive until the 1972 season, but they both played on varsity that year, the first year freshmen were eligible to do so.

All three would become All-Americans at Oklahoma. And in 1973, Lucious' senior season, No. 98 was flanked by his little brothers, both sophomores, in the Sooners' 3-5 defense. That season the trio of brothers accounted for 234 total tackles, 26 of those were for 139 yards in losses. Oklahoma, on NCAA probation, finished 10–0–1 and did not go to a bowl.

In the three seasons that Lee Roy and Dewey played together as starters (1973 to 1975), Oklahoma was 32–1–1 and won three Big 8 titles and two national championships.

"They were from the same mold, same character, all honor students, very coachable, great leaders," said former Oklahoma coach Barry Switzer. "Mom and Dad raised them right."

One fan during the 1973 season held a sign at an Oklahoma home game: "Thank You, Mrs. Selmon."

Billy Sims

Go to Heisman Park near Gaylord Family–Oklahoma Memorial Stadium and see the statue of one of OU's greatest runners. Then eat at one of Billy Sims' barbeque restaurants and maybe take a side trip to Hooks, Texas.

Sims, a fan favorite, was voted to the Orange Bowl Committee's 75-year team during the 2008 season. And on January 8, 2009, Billy Sims was back at the Orange Bowl and was being honored as the one former Heisman Trophy winner to play there during a 75th anniversary celebration. He displayed his high-stepping running motion during the pregame introductions and had the Sooners' partisans roaring.

Certainly, the Sooners that night could have used him as a runner when twice they were rebuffed near the goal line during the first half of a 24–14 loss to Florida for the national championship. They failed to get into the end zone on fourth down twice from the 1-yard line, and on another possession near the end of the first half, a pass (did we say pass in front of Barry Switzer?) was intercepted near the goal line.

A generation ago, Sims played in the actual Orange Bowl Stadium three straight seasons, from 1977 to 1979:

- In his first Orange Bowl appearance, on January 2, 1978, Sims actually fumbled early in the game as Arkansas jumped to a 14–0 lead and sailed to a 31–6 upset victory over OU. Sooners coach Barry Switzer called it "the most disappointing loss of my career." It possibly cost OU the national title.
- During his Heisman Trophy–winning junior season of 1978, Sims keyed a 31–24 OU victory over Big 8 rival

Go to a Billy Sims Barbecue Restaurant

Billy Sims has more than 30 restaurant locations in Oklahoma, Missouri, and Michigan. The restaurants offer a fun family atmosphere that highlights the career of one of Oklahoma's greatest running backs with photographs, jerseys, footballs, and other memorabilia. In 1995 Sims was inducted into the College Football Hall of Fame, and he has been involved in various business ventures since playing professional football.

"The restaurant is something I am very excited about," Sims said. "We've got a fun, family-oriented, tailgate kind of atmosphere, and some of the tastiest and most tender brisket and ribs around. It's truly a celebration of good food and good football—a place to kick back and enjoy yourself."

The restaurants are full of crimson and white items, as well as Detroit Lions' silver and blue. Sims was the No. 1 pick of the Lions in the 1980 NFL Draft, No. 1 overall, and played four and a half years for the Detroit franchise before a knee injury ended his career. He was named to the Pro Bowl three times.

A sampling from the menu: Bevo Plate (beef brisket), Pulled Razorback (pulled pork), Smoked Jayhawk (smoked chicken breast), and Turnover Turkey (smoked turkey breast). He serves "Okie Toast." Want the Heisman? It's chopped brisket or pulled pork with a slice of bologna and a hot link.

Nebraska in the Orange Bowl rematch of a regular-season game that the Sooners lost in Lincoln. He rushed for 134 yards on 25 carries and for two touchdowns. He was the game's offensive MVP.

- Sims led Oklahoma past Florida State as a senior in the 1980 Orange Bowl (24–7) with his 164-yard, one-touchdown performance, although OU quarterback J.C. Watts was named the offensive MVP.

The story is legendary of how Barry Switzer recruited Sims out of Hooks, Texas, with a phone call to him during halftime of a 49–14 blowout victory over Colorado during the 1974 national

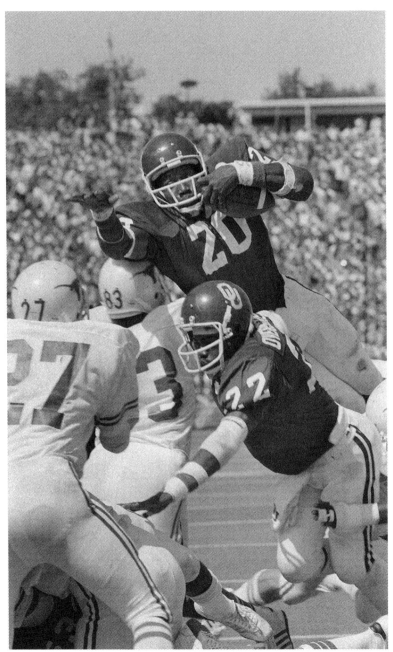

Billy Sims stretches for the end zone in an effort to score against Texas in Dallas on October 7, 1978.

championship season. He had to cut the conversation short when halftime ended, but added, "I got to go finish this butt-kicking."

The pitch worked. By the next season, Sims was in Norman, although his freshman and sophomore seasons and a redshirt year were wiped out by injuries. Finally, as a redshirt junior, No. 20 broke out with a Heisman Trophy season. Sims, about 30 years later, still holds the OU career record for rushing (4,118 yards). His 1978 OU single-season rushing record lasted more than a quarter of a century before Adrian Peterson eclipsed it in 2004.

In the 1978 season Sims led the nation in rushing and rushed for 200 yards in four games—Iowa State (231), Oklahoma State (209), Kansas State (202), and Colorado (221)—to win the 1978 Heisman Trophy over Penn State quarterback Chuck Fusina. As a senior in 1979, Sims rushed for more than 200 yards three times—Missouri (282), Nebraska (247), and Iowa State (202), but it wasn't good enough to win the Heisman. USC's Charles White was the nation's leading rusher and claimed the trophy.

Still, Sims' last two regular-season games against Missouri and Nebraska produced 529 yards combined and were very memorable. At the unveiling of Sims' statue at Heisman Park in Norman, on

Go to Hooks, Texas

Although Billy Sims grew up in the hardscrabble projects of St. Louis, Missouri, in the eighth grade he moved to Hooks, Texas, a town of around 3,000 people in northeast Texas, right on I-30. Hooks is only a few miles from the Arkansas border. Sims lived with his grandmother, Miss Sadie, and became a Texas high school football legend.

He rushed for at least 100 yards 38 straight times between 1972 and 1974, which is still a state record. He drew the attention of Switzer and other college coaches in Texas. People in the town can direct you to Billy Sims Road and the local library, where a wall is plastered with photos of Sims during his football career. Some old-timers may even know the station where he pumped gas, although more than 40 years years later the landscape has changed.

September 1, 2007, Switzer told the crowd gathered about a little visit he had with Sims. They were in the south end zone at Owen Field before what turned out to be a 17–14 victory over Nebraska, which propelled OU to a third straight Orange Bowl berth and 7–0 record in Big 8 play.

The coach and player reminisced about his career at OU. Switzer told him he probably would not win the Heisman Trophy. Switzer told the crowd, "I said, 'You got to give us the kind of game you had last week [against Missouri] to beat this bunch coming in.'"

Sims told him he had saved his best for last. And he had.

9 Game of the Century

It was OU's flamboyant wishbone with quarterback Jack Mildren at the controls and Greg Pruitt carrying the ball versus Jerry Tagge and Jeff Kinney doing the same in NU's I-formation attack. There were All–Big 8 Conference players galore in this game pitting the top two teams in college football, which had been on a collision course all season.

There was a difference of opinion just how the game would unfold. Both teams had spectacular defenses. Oklahoma certainly did not take a back seat in that department to Nebraska.

"We had some really good defensive players…Lucious Selmon and Derland Moore," said Jim Dickey, an assistant OU coach. "We knew when we went out there [in most games] we would win by a big score."

Had Oklahoma run a conventional offense (rather than the wishbone), Nebraska's outside linebackers or ends might have had an easier time, especially Willie Harper, who was a dynamic pass rusher.

"They were great [defensive] players," said Jim Walden, a Nebraska assistant at the time. "Harper had so much speed. Those were the wishbone years. Willie Harper was such a great pass rusher, he was so quick. But in the wishbone [which OU ran], you don't ever play a pass. You sit, sit, sit, and go out and play the quarterback or pitch. He would have loved to play in this era."

Sports Illustrated featured both teams on the cover, helmeted OU's Greg Pruitt and NU's Bob Terrio facing each other, with the headline: "Irresistible Oklahoma Meets Immovable Nebraska."

Oklahoma's 1971 Assistant Coaches

Chuck Fairbanks was the head coach of the 1971 Oklahoma team, which finished 11–1 and lost only to No. 1 Nebraska in the Game of the Century. After his career at Oklahoma, Fairbanks went on to coach the New England Patriots (1973–1978), the Colorado Buffaloes (1979–1981), and finally the New Jersey Generals of the United States Football League (1983). But he had an OU coaching staff in 1971 that included eight either future or former head coaches in either college football, the NFL, or both. Below is the listing of the assistant, his job in 1971 at OU, and where he was a head coach either before or after he was at Oklahoma.

Jim Dickey, Defensive Backs; Kansas State (1978–1985)
Galen Hall, Offensive Coordinator; Florida (1984–1989)
Bill Michael, Offensive Line; UTEP (1977–1981)
Warren Harper, Linebackers; UTEP (1963–1964)
Larry Lacewell, Defensive Coordinator; Arkansas State (1979–1989)
Jimmy Johnson, Defensive Line; Oklahoma State (1979–1983), Miami (Fla.) (1984–1988), Dallas Cowboys (1989–1993), Miami Dolphins (1996–1999)
Jerry Pettibone, Recruiting; Northern Illinois (1985–1990), Oregon State (1991–1996)
Barry Switzer, Assistant Head Coach; Oklahoma (1973–1988), Dallas Cowboys (1994–1997)

And with a national television audience on ABC watching, the atmosphere, on a gray day in Norman, was tense.

Nationally, Nebraska ranked in the top five in scoring defense, rushing defense, and total defense. But it had to rely on its offense this day, which averaged 437.7 yards a game.

Osborne, then an assistant coach, later said the Cornhuskers didn't know how to defend the Sooners' wishbone, and Oklahoma, likewise, couldn't stop Nebraska's potent attack. "We pretty much just ran up and down the field," Osborne said.

Nebraska struck first when Johnny Rodgers scored on a 72-yard punt return with 11:28 remaining in the first quarter for a 7–0 lead. This was the granddaddy of all punt returns and has been shown on television year after year.

Rodgers got out of a tackle by Pruitt and actually put a hand on the field to regain his balance. Although the Nebraska blocks in front of him were to the right, Rodgers zigged when maybe he should have zagged. He went left through a maze of OU players. All the Sooners missed him. He beat OU punter Joe Wylie, who was knocked out of the way by Nebraska's Joe Blahak.

"Even at that young age [11], I knew that was a football game," said Darrell Ray Dickey, son of Jim and a ball boy for OU at the time. "And, yes, there were three clips on Johnny Rodgers' punt return.... I saw them all, but what a great game!"

OU sliced Nebraska's lead to 7–3 on a field goal. Jeff Kinney scored on a one-yard run for a 14–3 Nebraska edge. Oklahoma quarterback Jack Mildren matched that with a rushing score of his own and threw a 24-yard pass for a 17–14 halftime lead.

The second half was more of the same drama. Kinney, on his way to a four-touchdown afternoon, scored twice in the third quarter to put Nebraska up 28–17. Then it was Mildren's turn again, with a three-yard touchdown run with 28 seconds remaining in the third quarter. The score stood, Nebraska 28, Oklahoma 24, entering the fourth quarter.

And then Mildren passed 16 yards to Jon Harrison with 7:10 left for a 31–28 OU lead.

There was one more drive left in the Cornhuskers.

"What I remember most, we scored, and they came right back down and beat us. It was a game where they were really good, and we were really good," Jim Dickey said. "They just beat us."

Tagge took Nebraska on a 74-yard drive for glory. Rodgers had a crucial 12-yard reception to keep the drive alive on a third-down play. Kinney ran the final two yards for a 35–31 victory with 1:38 remaining.

10 Joe Washington

At the Museum of the Gulf Coast, at 700 Procter Street, Port Arthur, Texas, you can actually see Joe Washington's famous silver shoes. There's also a bust of Washington, a statue of "Little Joe" running the ball, his OU helmet, a jersey, and several other items that Washington has donated to his hometown museum.

Come and celebrate the career of Washington, who was inducted into the College Football Hall of Fame in 2005 and today is executive director of the Varsity O Association at the University of Oklahoma. Four decades after he dazzled fans with his electric moves, Washington is still remembered for numerous big plays from 1972 to 1975 and during the Sooners' run to national titles in 1974 and 1975.

During Washington's four seasons in 46 career games, Oklahoma was 43–2–1 as he zoomed to the head of the Oklahoma career rushing charts with 4,071 yards. He ran for 39 touchdowns.

Joe Washington leaps high for a first down against the Longhorns in Dallas on October 12, 1974.

Oklahoma coach Barry Switzer has called Washington his "greatest player." Certainly from very early on, Switzer knew what he had. Washington pranced upon the scene and immediately made an impact when he went 80 yards for a touchdown in his first scrimmage as a freshman in 1972 against the Sooners' first-string defensive line.

The running style of the 5'8", 180-pound Washington was described by Texas coach Darrell Royal once as "smoother than smoke through a key hole." That quote reflected Washington's ability to slither through holes and then turn on the afterburners and go the distance. This was most apparent during a 1975 game at Missouri, when the Sooners were trailing 27–20 in the fourth quarter. Washington, on a fourth-and-one play, went 71 yards for a score and ran for two points on the conversion in a 28–27 victory. Switzer also calls the touchdown run the greatest play during his tenure at OU because the Sooners wouldn't have won the national championship without it.

"Little Joe was fascinating, the way he cut back across the grain because he could run sideways as fast as he could forward," said Dean Blevins, who was an OU quarterback on that team. "He got past one [defender], slipped under another, and the next thing you know, he was into secondary, and they just didn't catch him."

Little Joe, an All-American in 1974 and 1975, could do it all:

- He threw a 40-yard halfback option pass to split end Tinker Owens in 1973 in the first half of a 52–13 rout of Texas in Dallas.
- In 1973 during the one tie game in his OU career, in his sophomore season against USC, he may have run 50 yards to gain nine in a zig-zagging punt return at the L.A. Coliseum. The 7–7 game is available online.
- In a 1974 game against Oklahoma State, Washington's 57-yard punt return for a touchdown sent the Sooners on their way to a 44–13 victory over the Cowboys.
- In 1975 his 76-yard punt, yes punt, on a quick-kick against Texas pinned the Longhorns deep in their own territory and preserved a 24–17 OU victory.

Upon leaving OU, Washington was the fourth overall pick in the 1976 NFL Draft by the San Diego Chargers and played nine seasons in the NFL with four different teams—San Diego, Baltimore, Washington, and Atlanta. He was inducted into the Oklahoma Sports Hall of Fame in 1993, during which time he thanked the flamboyant Switzer for allowing him to wear his spray-painted silver shoes that he had donned in high school and then eventually wore at OU. Twelve years later he was inducted into the College Football Hall of Fame.

11 1955 National Title Team

Bud Wilkinson's second national championship was sandwiched between two other unbeaten seasons and in the middle of the 47-game winning streak, which has been immortalized in numerous books. The Sooners' dynasty was one of the greatest of all time, and the winning streak is unparalleled in major-college football history in terms of the number of games.

The Sooners entered the 1955 season with a 19-game winning streak dating to a 7–7 tie at Pittsburgh in the second game of the 1953 season. They went through the 1954 season unblemished and were ranked No. 1 in four of the first five polls. Ohio State and UCLA eventually finished ahead of the Sooners, who finished third in both AP and UPI polls.

In 1955 UCLA started as the No. 1 team. Jim Tatum's Maryland team also was ranked in the top spot, but eventually it was the Sooners who would win the first of two straight national titles. Unlike the 1950 team, these Sooners were dominant. They gave up only 54 points during the regular season and just six in their Orange Bowl victory over Maryland—which still didn't figure into their national title because the final poll had been

OU Winning Streaks

Oklahoma has the longest winning streak in major-college football history of 47 games, from 1953 to 1957, under Bud Wilkinson. But the Sooners also have another winning streak of 31 straight games under Wilkinson, from 1948 to 1950, which ranks among the top 10 all-time among major schools. And there's a third winning streak of 28 straight games, from 1973 to 1975, under Barry Switzer, which is among the top 20 all-time.

Streak	Loss/Tie	Streak Starter (win)	Streak Ender (loss)
47 straight	7–7 tie (Pitt)	Texas 19–14	Notre Dame 7–0
31 straight	20–17 (Santa Clara)	Texas A&M 42–14	Kentucky 13–7
28 straight	7–7 tie (USC)	Miami 24–20	Kansas 23–3

conducted—but it did reaffirm OU's position as college football's best team.

Despite OU's dominance during this period, the Sooners never led an Associated Press poll from start to finish during a complete regular season—odd but true. And they still haven't during their entire history.

The 1955 Oklahoma team, led by College Football Hall of Famers linebacker-center-fullback Jerry Tubbs and halfback "Shoo-Fly" Tommy McDonald, rolled up fantastic offensive numbers. Tubbs had been moved from fullback to center in 1955. The Sooners led the country in total offense (410.7 yards), in rushing offense (328.9 yards a game), and in scoring offense (36.5 ppg). Jimmy Harris was the quarterback in the split-T.

"Split-T, it was a great offense because the quarterback would keep the ball and flip it back to you," said the speedy and wiry McDonald. "I could use my speed and take off and run. It was really fantastic."

And the defense wasn't bad, either. Oklahoma shut out five opponents that season—Texas (20–0), Missouri (20–0), Iowa State

(52–0), Nebraska (41–0), and Oklahoma State (53–0)—the last four in succession to end the regular season.

Oklahoma, by this time, was so dominant in the Big 7 Conference that other teams were wondering if they could ever keep up with the Sooners' machine. Oklahoma placed seven players on the consensus Big 7 All-Conference for the first of two straight seasons. Besides Tubbs and McDonald, tackles Ed Gray and Cal Woodworth, guards Bo Bolinger and Cecil Morris, and back Bob Burris were all-league.

Bolinger, who finished ninth in the Heisman Trophy balloting as a senior, was also a consensus All-American in 1955 and was a member of a group of players on that Oklahoma team known as the "B Boys." The others were center-linebacker Kurt Burris, back Bob Burris, and end Max Boydston. All four hailed from Muskogee, Oklahoma. Boydston and Kurt Burris were All-Americans as well, with Burris finishing runner-up to Wisconsin fullback Alan Ameche in the 1954 Heisman Trophy race.

During the 1955 season, Oklahoma's closest game was a season-opening 13–6 victory over North Carolina in Chapel Hill. But this team had too much speed for Big 7 teams and rival Texas. Potential Big 7 showdowns with Missouri and Nebraska were hardly that. Oklahoma finished as the No. 1–ranked team, beating out No. 2 and once-beaten Michigan State. At No. 3, Maryland was 10–0–0 and in a position to threaten the Sooners in the Orange Bowl, but after his Sooners trailed 6–0 at halftime, Wilkinson went to a hurry-up offense in the second half, and the Sooners registered their 30th straight victory, 20–6.

"One thing about Wilkinson, he would come up with different stuff," McDonald said. "That was one of the things he had for the University of Maryland. We didn't do that during the season, but we surprised them with his hurry-up offense. We didn't even give them time to get in the huddle to call defensive plays."

During one second-half drive, Oklahoma ran three plays in 38 seconds. McDonald scored on a four-yard run. Then on another series, Oklahoma ran 16 plays in hurried fashion and scored to go up 14–6 and in command. Two OU pass interceptions in the second half—one by Tubbs and the other by Carl Dodd, which turned into an 82-yard return for a touchdown—doused any talk the Terrapins should have been No. 1. "That's the most satisfying victory we ever had," Wilkinson said.

12 Oklahoma-Georgia Lawsuit

The Oklahoma Historical Society, at 2401 North Laird Avenue, Oklahoma City, possesses one of the most important lawsuits in college football history in their database of *the Daily Oklahoman*. Reporter Jerry McConnell did most of the coverage when the Sooners took on the NCAA.

When you mention Oklahoma-Georgia, it's not about a football game. In fact, oddly enough, the two teams have never met on the football field. But they were on the same side in a lawsuit against the NCAA that completely altered college football television more than 25 years ago.

From 1953 to 1983, the NCAA controlled the national airwaves with an iron grip, setting the times, limiting the number of television games on Saturdays, and restricting the number of live television appearances a college football team could have over specified periods. During this time, Oklahoma was never on live television more than three times in a season, starting with its first appearance on NBC against Notre Dame in 1952. The NCAA had become concerned in the early 1950s that Notre Dame, the dominant team in the late 1940s and early 1950s, would dominate the airwaves because of its association with NBC, known affectionately as the "Notre Dame Broadcast Company." Other super powers would do the same, the NCAA said. This would create a competitive imbalance in the sport.

The NCAA took control of regular-season television and put in its appearance rules, which often kept the best games off television or rerouted less appealing games into various markets. A SWAC or Ivy League game could have the same rights fees paid to the schools through the NCAA program as, say, Arkansas-Texas. And the NCAA guaranteed the less powerful conferences a certain number of television appearances.

Eventually in the early 1980s the College Football Association was formed, and Chuck Neinas, a former NCAA employee and Big 8 Conference commissioner from 1971 to 1980, was named its executive director. All major conferences (and Notre Dame), except the Big Ten and Pac-10, were members of the CFA, which was viewed as a rules-lobbying group with the NCAA. But major

Swinging Gate Beats Army

Oklahoma started out the 1961 season 0–5, which is the worst start in Sooners football history. But Bud Wilkinson rallied his team for a November to remember. The Sooners won four straight games during that month and a fifth against Oklahoma State in early December to finish 5–5. Included in the November games was a 14–8 victory over Army at Yankee Stadium before 37,000 people and an ABC regional television audience.

In scouting the Black Knights, Wilkinson had noticed that Army's defensive players were slow getting to the line of scrimmage. So he devised a play where Oklahoma would go with no-huddle. The OU quarterback quickly took the snap and made a long lateral to running back Mike McClellan. With a fleet of blockers, he dashed 75 yards down the sideline for a 7–0 OU lead. McClellan came dangerously close to the sideline and swiping an ABC hand-held camera.

schools, frustrated with the NCAA appearance rules and eyeing potential revenue, eventually revolted. In 1981 Oklahoma president Bill Banowsky and the Oklahoma Board of Regents, plus the Georgia Athletic Association, were the leaders in this revolt.

The two CFA member schools jointly filed a lawsuit against the NCAA for restraint of trade (Sherman Anti-Trust) in Federal Court in Oklahoma City. A year later U.S. Federal Court justice Juan Burciaga ruled the NCAA had acted like a "classic cartel" in violating antitrust laws. Two years later, in 1984, the U.S. Supreme Court upheld Burciaga's decision. The NCAA was out of the college football television business.

For about a 10-year period, the CFA had a college football television plan. And the Big Ten and Pac-10 had plans. Eventually, Notre Dame and all the individual conferences began running their own plans with various television networks and cable outlets. The Fighting Irish were back on NBC every week, the same network that televised that OU–Notre Dame game from South Bend in 1952.

In 1984, after college football television was deregulated from NCAA control, Oklahoma had eight regular-season games on television. Now, every Oklahoma games is on some kind of network or cable.

13 1974 National Title Team

In only his second season as head coach, Barry Switzer did what the three previous Sooner head coaches—Jim Mackenzie, Gomer Jones, and Chuck Fairbanks—couldn't do in the preceding decade. Switzer won a national championship—according to the Associated

Press Writers' poll—although the Sooners were on NCAA probation and ineligible to go to a bowl for a second straight season and did not appear on live television.

Oklahoma also was ineligible to be ranked in the United Press International poll, the coaches' poll. Thusly, Southern California, at 10–1–1, was selected as national champion by the coaches.

Despite the fact the Sooners were treated like college football outcasts and banned from television during the 1974 season and from bowls in 1973 and 1974, Switzer was nearly perfect in his first two seasons, with only a tie at USC in his second game to spoil his first 22 games as head coach. At the end of Switzer's second season, OU had run its unbeaten streak to 29 games, including winning the final seven games of the 1972 season, when Chuck Fairbanks was head coach and Switzer was an assistant coach.

The 1974 team (11–0) had eight All-Americans, the most of any OU team until that point. It was led by All-America split end Tinker Owens (Steve's brother) and halfback Joe Washington, both juniors, and senior All-America offensive linemen, guard John Roush and center Kyle Davis. On the defensive side of the ball, senior linebacker Rod Shoate and defensive back Randy Hughes joined two of the Selmon brothers, Lee Roy and Dewey, as All-Americans.

Roush, who was an Academic All-American as well, summed up what allowed him to reach the pinnacle of success as a lineman: "I had to block them [the Selmons and Shoate] when I was on the scout team. Whew!" Playing in the games was easy after that for Roush, who was a leading blocker in the wishbone offense directed by Steve Davis, the ever-polite but still ruthlessly effective son of a Baptist minister.

In 1974 the Sooners hurled three shutouts, including a 37–0 smashing of Missouri in Norman. That was one of their better defensive efforts, coming against a team that beat Nebraska that season in Lincoln. In 11 games, no team scored more than two

OU All-America Brothers

There have been three brother All-America combinations in the history of Oklahoma football.

Selmons from Eufaula, Oklahoma
*Lee Roy Selmon, DT (1974, 1975)
Dewey Selmon, NG (1974, 1975)
Lucious Selmon, NG (1973)

Burrises from Muskogee, Oklahoma
+Buddy Burris, G (1946, 1947, 1948)
Kurt Burris, C (1954)

Owenses from Miami, Oklahoma
Steve Owens, HB (1968, 1969)
Tinker Owens, SE (1974)

*Outland Trophy Winner (Best Interior Lineman in College Football)
+One of two three-time All-Americans at OU. LB Rod Shoate (1972–1974) is the other.

touchdowns against Oklahoma. The closest game was a 16–13 decision over Texas in Dallas in which Washington had 122 yards rushing.

The electrifying Washington had his biggest rushing season in 1974, when he bolted for 1,321 yards and 12 touchdowns, with a 6.8 yards a carry average. Washington's nifty moves allowed him to cut back against the grain and baffle opponents. The 5'11", 168-pound Tinker Owens was a receiving complement to Washington and caught 18 passes for 413 yards, an average of 22.9 yards a catch.

The 1974 Oklahoma team will go down as one of the school's greatest ever, although hardly anyone in America outside of the Big 8 Conference saw it because of the television and bowl ban. Three of the Sooners' four nonconference games were at home, and OU won by a combined score of 163–14 over Baylor (28–11), Utah State (72–3), and Wake Forest (63–0) to start the historic season.

One of the biggest plays of the season was pulled off by receiver Billy Brooks, a 40-yard touchdown on a reverse to pull OU even with Texas 13–13 in Dallas. A field goal late in the game provided the difference in OU's closest game of the season.

Quarterback Steve Davis led an offense that led the nation in scoring (43.0 points a game), in total offense (507.7 yards a game), and in rushing offense (438.8 yards a game). It was the third time in four seasons Oklahoma had led the country in rushing. The Sooners' 73.9 rushing attempts a game is still an NCAA record. In what amounted to the Big 8 title game, Oklahoma didn't complete a pass against Nebraska, but still won 28–14.

14 2000 National Title Team

The Bob Stoops era began at Oklahoma with modest success in 1999: a 7–4 regular-season record and a trip to the Independence Bowl, where OU dropped a 27–25 decision to Ole Miss. But anything looked good to Sooners fans at that point—after five straight seasons without a winning record and just one bowl trip under three different head coaches, Gary Gibbs, Howard Schnellenberger, and John Blake.

Little did anyone know Stoops' first season, however modest, would serve as a springboard for OU's seventh national title in 2000. The initial campaign allowed Stoops to instill his discipline, harness the promising talent left by Blake, and insert junior college transfer Josh Heupel as his quarterback.

"When we arrived at Oklahoma, it was pretty well noted that we just didn't have a strong self-image, to be honest with you," Stoops said before the 2009 Orange Bowl. "And I felt as a program we were shying away from those expectations. And I remember telling the players in maybe one of our first meetings, and I kept showing them some of the championship teams and said, 'This is what we are supposed to be.'

"I look at Bud Wilkinson and Barry Switzer. And I said, 'I have to walk by those guys on the way to my office every day, life-sized paintings of them.... This is what we're supposed to be and this is how we are supposed to play. It's my job, and I am not shying away from the expectations of Oklahoma.... I look back at that 2000 group. I don't know if we had any business winning it [the national title]. But they thought we did.'"

The 2000 team opened with a 55–14 victory over UTEP and hammered Texas 63–14 in Dallas in what was the first of five straight victories over the Longhorns. By the time the season was over, Heupel, in his brief two-year career at OU, had passed for 7,456 yards and 53 touchdowns and was the Heisman runner-up to Florida State's Chris Weinke, who would lose to OU in the Orange Bowl.

Oklahoma's closest regular-season game was a 35–31 victory at Texas A&M. Linebacker Torrance Marshall's 41-yard interception return for a touchdown won the game for the Sooners, who trailed the Aggies 31–21 with just eight minutes remaining in the game.

Oklahoma beat Kansas State 27–24 when Tim Duncan made a career-long 46-yard field goal with 1:25 to play. At the Orange Bowl, Oklahoma authored a 13–2 defensive masterpiece against the Seminoles. It was the lowest-scoring Orange Bowl since Penn State defeated Missouri 10–3 in 1970.

Oklahoma finished as the nation's only unbeaten team, claimed No. 1 in the Associated Press poll, and was automatically named No. 1 in the coaches' poll after winning the Orange Bowl. Marshall was selected the Orange Bowl's Most Outstanding Player. Another linebacker, Rocky Calmus, forced a Weinke fumble that led to the clinching touchdown. Only an FSU safety in the final minute prevented Florida State's first shutout in 12 seasons.

Another star of the 2000 team was All-America defensive back-returner J.T. Thatcher, who had eight interceptions and nearly 900 return yards on special teams his final season.

15 Bennie Owen

The University of Oklahoma's field is named after former coach Bennie Owen, principally because he was the heart and soul of the program for the first quarter of the 20th century. He became the first Sooners football coach to serve for more than four seasons, beat Texas for the first time, 2–0 in 1905, and created the fan interest that led to the building of the Sooners' Memorial Stadium in the mid-1920s.

Through the 2013 season, Owen still has the longest tenure of any Oklahoma head football coach: 22 seasons. He is one of four coaches in OU history to win 100 games at the school. Bud Wilkinson, Barry Switzer, and Bob Stoops are the others.

After compiling a 122–54–16 record at Oklahoma, Owen was the first person associated with the Oklahoma football program to be inducted into the College Football Hall of Fame, in 1951, the Hall's inaugural class. Owen doubled as Oklahoma's basketball coach for 13 seasons, from 1908–1909 through 1920–1921, and won nearly 70 percent of his games.

Originally a quarterback for the Kansas Jayhawks in 1898 and then again in 1899 (10–0) in coach Fielding Yost's only season in Lawrence, Owen coached one season under Yost at Michigan in 1901, when the Wolverines won the first of four straight national

Jim Tatum, Biff Jones: Hall of Famers

Jim Tatum coached only one season at Oklahoma (1946) and Biff Jones only two (1935 and 1936). But they made their names at other schools and were inducted into the College Football Hall of Fame 30 years apart. Jones went in to the Hall in 1954 and Tatum in 1984.

In 1937 Jones left Oklahoma for Nebraska. He compiled only a 9–6–3 overall record at OU, but was more successful at other stops— Army, LSU, and Nebraska, which he took to the Rose Bowl after the 1940 season. Tatum got a pay raise to go to Maryland after leading Oklahoma to the Gator Bowl in 1946 where the Sooners beat North Carolina State. Tatum was 73–15–4 at Maryland and won the national title in 1953. He spent his last three seasons, 1956 through 1958, coaching at his alma mater, North Carolina.

titles. As a prelude of things to come in Norman, Owen was exposed to Yost's hurry-up offense that outscored opponents 550–0 in 1901.

On his way to OU, Owen was head coach at Bethany College (Kansas) from 1902 through 1904 and posted two victories over the Sooners, 12–10 in 1903 and 36–9 in 1904. But Owen reversed that in 1905, when the Sooners beat Bethany on the way to a 7–2 season. At the time, it was the most victories for the Sooners in a season since the football program debuted in 1895.

Owen was a disciple of the forward pass in a time when the "Father of College Football," Walter Camp, would have liked to have done away with passing. Owen used the pass and had his best teams between 1911 and 1920, when OU posted such point totals of 140, 179, and 157. Owen brought in smaller, faster players who could outrun bigger, more physical teams. He also took advantage of the new college rules that allowed more deception in the running game—the first back taking the snap from center could run between the tackles.

The Sooners' high-scoring teams had four unbeaten seasons during that era: 8–0 in 1911, 10–0 in 1915, 6–0 in 1918, and 6–0–1 in 1920. Under Owen, the university recognized its first

All-Conference player, back Owen Acton (1907), and the first two All-Americans, passing fullbacks Claude Reeds (1913) and Spot Geyer (1915). In 1914 Oklahoma went 9–1–1 and led the country in scoring.

In October 1907 Owen lost his right arm in a hunting accident and missed the rest of a 4–4 season. He even survived a possible ouster when there was a change of athletics directors and there were those who believed his salary was excessive. But his pleasant nature was loved by his players, and he was considered an example of sportsmanship.

Owen was a driving fund-raising force in the development of Memorial Stadium in the 1920s and a basketball field house. The first game was played on the site of Memorial Stadium in 1923. By 1925, 16,000 seats were erected on the west side of the field as Memorial Stadium began to take shape. Another 16,000 seats were added on the east side in time for the 1929 season.

After ending his coaching career, Owen remained as athletics director for several years. He died in 1970 at age 94.

16 Sam Bradford

In 2008 Sam Bradford became the Sooners' fifth Heisman Trophy winner when he smashed many of OU's single-season passing records. The no-huddle offense, with Bradford in control, produced a Big 12 Conference title and a modern-day record of five straight games scoring at least 60 points—against Nebraska, Texas A&M, Texas Tech, Oklahoma State, and Missouri.

"Everybody knows [Bradford] as being quiet," said OU running back Chris Brown. "But he is a vocal leader also. He complements the team. He keeps us up. If we have a three-and-out drive, he keeps us coming back and gives us motivation to get something going on the next drive. I think that plays a big part in everybody's confidence."

Bradford, from Putnam City North High School, was a second-generation Sooner (his father Kent lettered as an OU offensive lineman in 1977–1978). Sam Bradford is also a member of the Cherokee Tribe. A finance major, he was a CoSIDA Academic All-America and one of the smartest and most efficient quarterbacks in NCAA history.

"The guy is talented," Oklahoma coach Bob Stoops said. "He is incredibly bright. He's competitive. He's tough. He's everything you look for. And then you look at his production...."

This led Stoops to an important decision entering the 2008 season, which allowed Bradford to win the Heisman Trophy and become only the second sophomore at the time to do so after Florida quarterback Tim Tebow.

"I felt with the emergence and the cool and calm nature of Sam, and having a year of experience and the way he handled everything a year ago, I felt he would handle it really well," Stoops said of Oklahoma going to the no-huddle offense. "The experience of our offensive personnel was a positive."

In 2008 Bradford led the nation in touchdown passes (50) and in passing efficiency.

Bradford's 4,720 yards passing that season are the most at OU in a single season, as are his 300-yard passing games (11) in a season.

After his sophomore season, Bradford had passed for 7,841 yards and trailed only OU's previous Heisman Trophy winner, Jason White, with 7,922 yards, in the school's record books.

Bradford elected to stay for his junior season rather than enter the NFL Draft. But in the 2009 season opener against BYU at the

An unassuming, second-generation Sooner, Sam Bradford rewrote Oklahoma's quarterback record book.

Dallas Cowboys' new stadium in Arlington, Texas, he suffered a shoulder injury that knocked him out of the game.

Bradford returned four weeks later to lead the Sooners to a 33–7 victory over Baylor. But against Texas on October 17, his season ended when he re-injured the shoulder. Oklahoma lost that game and struggled to an 8–5 record the rest of the season. This time Bradford elected to leave OU with a year of eligibility remaining. He was the No. 1 overall pick by the St. Louis Rams in the 2010 draft and was rookie of the year.

17 1975 National Title Team

In 1975 the defending national champion Sooners were finally off NCAA probation and eligible for postseason play. The NCAA television ban would be lifted for the bowl game. Riding a 29-game unbeaten streak, the Sooners actually had won 20 straight games since the 7–7 tie against USC early in the 1973 season.

Halfback Joe Washington returned for his senior season, along with split ends Tinker Owens and Billy Brooks. And they provided the offensive punch again. Lee Roy Selmon would win the Outland Trophy, and his brother Dewey Selmon, a nose guard, also collected All-America honors that season.

One sequence of plays saved the season in the 10th game at Missouri. The Sooners' 28–27 victory hinged on Washington's long touchdown scamper and two-point conversion run that rallied the Sooners late in the game. Missouri had trailed 20–0 at halftime, before storming back in the second half to take a 27–20 lead.

"It was a very important game at Missouri because we had lost to Kansas the week before," Lee Roy Selmon said.

Lee Roy Selmon grimaces as he puts on a helmet while holding an Orange Bowl program in his teeth during picture day on December 26, 1975, in Miami. Oklahoma played the University of Michigan in the 1976 Orange Bowl on New Year's Day.

The Sooners won their first eight games of the 1975 season, although they had three close calls in a row—a 20–17 road victory at Miami (Fla.), a 21–20 home victory over Colorado, and the annual blood bath with Texas in Dallas, 24–17. They slipped from the No. 1 ranking because of those performances, but they had gobbled up the rest of the Big 8 entering Week 9 against Kansas in Norman. And they were riding a 28-game winning streak, unbeaten in 37 straight games.

Behind quarterback Nolan Cromwell, KU shocked the college football world with a 23–3 victory over the Sooners in Norman. A decathlete, Cromwell ran around, through, and over the bewildered Sooners, who hadn't lost at home since the 1971 Game of the Century against Nebraska. OU's loss strengthened the Ohio State Buckeyes' grip on the No. 1 ranking in the AP poll.

It was the first time in 103 games that Oklahoma had failed to score a touchdown—since the Sooners had lost 38–0 to Notre Dame in South Bend on October 22, 1966, during Jim Mackenzie's only season as head coach.

A loss to Missouri surely would have taken the Sooners out of the national championship race. But with Little Joe and Sooner Magic, they prevailed—barely—in Columbia when a late Missouri field goal, which could have won the game, went astray.

In the final game of the regular season, Oklahoma routinely beat Nebraska 35–10 to tie the Cornhuskers for the Big 8 Conference title and earn a trip to face Michigan in the Orange Bowl as the league's representative. The Wolverines had lost to top-ranked Ohio State, which was playing in the Rose Bowl.

As luck would have it, the Buckeyes stumbled to UCLA in the Rose Bowl, and No. 3 Oklahoma beat Michigan 14–6, to win Switzer his second national title. With the Sooners off probation, Oklahoma was crowned champion in the UPI poll, making a sweep of the two major polls.

There were eight All-Americans on this team: the two Selmons, Washington, Owens, Brooks, guard Terry Webb, tackle Mike Vaughan, and defensive end Jimbo Elrod.

18 1985 National Title Team

Although the mid-1970s national title teams under Switzer were known as great defensive teams, the mid-1980s OU teams were actually among the best in the country in the four major defensive statistical categories and led in several areas.

From 1984 through 1987 Oklahoma was simply brilliant on the defensive side of the ball under defensive coordinator Gary Gibbs. From 1985 through 1987 Oklahoma led the nation in total defense. In 1984 and 1986 OU led all major schools in rushing defense. From 1985 through 1987 the Sooners led the country in pass defense. And in both 1986 and 1987 OU was tops in scoring defense—allowing only about a touchdown a game each season.

This was a remarkable set of defensive statistics for a team playing in a major conference.

From 1984 through 1987 Oklahoma compiled a 42–5–1 record, won (in 1984 tied with Nebraska) four straight Big 8 titles, and played in four consecutive Orange Bowls. During that four-year stretch, three of OU's losses came to Miami (Fla.), two during regular-season games in 1985 and 1986 and the other in the January 1, 1988, Orange Bowl. The latter victory by Miami propelled the Hurricanes to the national title over the top-ranked Sooners, who were unbeaten going into the bowl game.

Former Oklahoma State coach Jimmy Johnson may have taken his lumps during the Bedlam Series, from 1979 to 1983, when his Oklahoma State team lost five straight games to the Sooners. But he got his revenge coaching Miami in the three high-profile games between the Hurricanes and Sooners, which all had national-title implications.

The 1985 team was the only OU team of the era to win the national title, which it earned after beating No. 1 Penn State 25–10 in the Orange Bowl. The Sooners were able to overcome a 27–14 defeat in Norman to Miami early in the season.

The defensive stars of the era were lineman Tony Casillas, linebacker Brian Bosworth, ends Darrell Reed and Kevin Murphy, defensive back Rickey Dixon, and linebacker Danté Jones. Bosworth, Casillas, and Murphy were all All-Americans during the 1985 national-title season after Murphy had been granted an extra

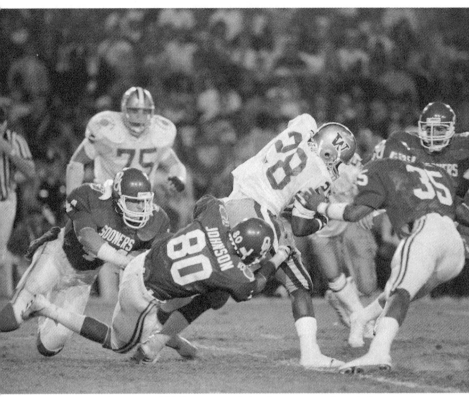

From 1984 to 1987 Oklahoma compiled a 42–5–1 record, including this loss in the Orange Bowl on January 1, 1985. Here, Washington's Jacque Robinson is tackled by a posse of Sooners defenders, including Brian Bosworth, Troy Johnson (80), Tony Rayburn (35), and Dante Jones.

year of eligibility because of an early season injury in 1984. And they were defensive terrors in the Midlands.

Bosworth was a tackling machine and won the first two Butkus Awards (given to the best linebacker in college football) in 1985 and 1986. Through the 2008 college football season, nearly a quarter of a century later, he is still the only two-time winner of that award. Casillas claimed the 1985 Lombardi Award for the country's best linemen. OU coaches said Casillas had the fastest feet they had ever seen and that they moved like a "sewing machine." He was a dominant pass rusher. Switzer called him perhaps the best defensive lineman ever at OU.

In 1985 only rival Miami (Fla.) was able to score more than 14 points against OU. Miami topped this benchmark in its 27–14 win in Norman. Eight teams scored seven points or less against what usually was an impregnable OU defense.

Maybe the most impressive performance was a 14–7 victory over Texas in which the Sooners held the Longhorns to just four first downs and 70 yards of total offense.

"This was the greatest defensive performance by an Oklahoma team since I have been here, and that's 20 years, including the time I was an assistant," said Oklahoma coach Barry Switzer.

19 Prentice Gautt

The Prentice Gautt Learning Center at the north end of Gaylord Family–Oklahoma Memorial Stadium is a great academic aid to Sooners athletes as well as a memorial to a player who helped the school achieve racial diversity.

In 1956 coach Bud Wilkinson made the move to integrate the Oklahoma football team when a group of African American doctors and pharmacists in Oklahoma City indicated that Prentice Gautt, a star running back at all-black Douglass High School, would be the player to do it.

Gautt had played in the first integrated high school football game in Oklahoma and was the first African American in the state's all-star football game. He was also president of his senior class and a member of the National Honor Society. And in 1957 he became the first African American to play football for the Sooners.

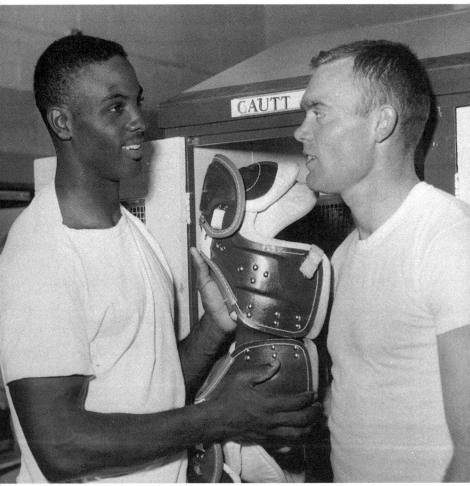

Prentice Gautt, who in 1956 became the first black football player at Oklahoma and went on to play in the NFL, speaks with teammate Brewster Hobby in September 1957.

Gautt was Oklahoma's leading rusher in 1958 and 1959 and was All–Big 8 Conference his junior and senior seasons. He also scored the first touchdown when Oklahoma beat Syracuse in the January 1, 1959, Orange Bowl 21–6, and was the Game's Most Outstanding Player. He was an Academic All-American as a senior.

"This was a guy, in Bud [Wilkinson's] mind, who could withstand all the crap that he would take," said National Football Foundation executive director Steve Hatchell, who worked with Gautt at the Big 8 Conference office from 1979 to 1983. "Bud said he didn't realize there would be as much of it as there was. He knew there would be some. But there was a lot, especially when they traveled. Prentice said once he got on campus, the campus atmosphere was pretty cool. Everybody embraced Prentice. When they traveled, it was pretty ugly. Sitting on buses and the taunts at games were pretty rough stuff."

Initially Gautt's scholarship was paid for by the doctors and pharmacists, but two months into his freshman year, Wilkinson put him on athletic scholarship, and the money was given to another African American student.

But when Gautt was a freshman at Oklahoma, he was denied a place to eat at a restaurant when the team's bus stopped on the way back to Norman. Gautt, who passed away in March 2005, related the story to Hatchell several years ago.

"As they walked in the door, the owner of the restaurant grabbed Prentice gently by the arm and said, 'We have a place for you to eat, but you can't eat with the team,'" Hatchell recalled Gautt telling him. "The place he had for him to eat was actually downstairs in the basement. At first, it didn't hit Prentice what the guy was saying. He thought a bunch of guys had to go downstairs or whatever."

Gautt ignored him a couple of times. But when the owner of the restaurant persisted, Prentice got up and threw his napkin down. He told his teammates he would wait on the bus for the team.

"Another great player got up on a chair and said, 'They won't let Prentice eat in here with us,'" Hatchell said. "'We have two choices. We can stay here and eat, and I know we are all hungry. We can get back on the bus and get burgers.' The team packed up and left."

The Prentice Gautt Academic Center

Located in the north end of Gaylord Family–Oklahoma Memorial Stadium, the Prentice Gautt Academic Center has 35,000 square feet devoted to the academic pursuits of Sooners athletes. The center is available more than 90 hours a week and has a computer lab of more than 100 units for Oklahoma's athletes and 100 laptops that can be checked out. It was dedicated in 1999 and has helped Oklahoma student-athletes, who complete their eligibility to an 84 percent graduation rate.

After his Oklahoma career, Gautt was selected by the Cleveland Browns in the second round of the 1960 NFL Draft and played eight seasons of professional ball, mostly with the St. Louis Cardinals. He later received his doctorate degree in counseling psychology at the University of Missouri while assisting the Tigers football team and then moved over to the university's faculty. He went to work for the Big 8 Conference office as an assistant commissioner in 1979 and stayed with the league, later the Big 12, until his death.

"His ability to relate to people was his best quality," said Bill Hancock. "He never met anybody he didn't like. I don't think people of our generation can understand what it was like in Oklahoma in 1956. It took a special person to deal with that."

"It is almost impossible to describe his personality," Hatchell added. "Prentice was so incredibly down to earth and he was so smart, he could see through prejudice. Education was so important to him. And if you had to rate listeners in the world, he might be one of the top four or five."

20 1950 National Title Team

It's the first of Oklahoma's seven national championships listed on the back of the Oklahoma scoreboard at Gaylord Family–Oklahoma Memorial Stadium. In coach Bud Wilkinson's fourth season as head coach, the Sooners for the first time had climbed to the mountaintop of college football.

Wilkinson had been promoted from Jim Tatum's staff when Tatum left for Maryland after one season and promptly directed the Sooners to 7–2–1, 10–1, and 11–0 seasons from 1947 through 1949 with a collection of war veterans brought into Norman.

Entering the 1950 season, Oklahoma was actually on a 21-game winning streak dating to a 20–17 loss at Santa Clara to begin the 1948 season. After that loss, the Sooners won their next 10 games of the 1948 season and were a perfect 11–0 in 1949. They had been building to the point they could wrest the national title away from the likes of national powers Army and Notre Dame, either of which had won every AP poll national title except one—Michigan in 1948—from 1943 to 1949.

In Tatum's only season in Norman, the Sooners finished 14th in the final 1946 AP poll. In 1947 Wilkinson's first team tied Kansas for the old Big 6 title and still was able to climb to a No. 16 rating. Then came AP top five finishes in 1948 and 1949, setting the stage for the 1950 team. That team was led by All-America senior full-back Leon Heath, a tough inside runner in the split-T, and junior lineman Jim Weatherall, a then-massive 6'4", 230-pounder who would win the Outland Trophy in 1951.

Ironically, OU's first national championship in 1950 had a blemish on its record, a 13–7 loss to Bear Bryant's Kentucky team in the Sugar Bowl on January 1, 1951. In those days, the national champion was crowned before the bowl games. Thus, at 10–0, Wilkinson's Sooners won the top prize, although their 31-game winning streak was snapped by the Wildcats, who took a 13–0 halftime lead and confused OU with a three-man defensive tackle front.

"That was a pretty hard loss to take," said OU's future Outland Trophy winner lineman J.D. Roberts, who was just a freshman that season. "I was listening to it on the radio. We didn't have a TV in our house. I know we moved the ball well. We just got down there and made too many errors."

During the 1950 season Army, Notre Dame, SMU, and Ohio State all were ranked No. 1 before Oklahoma took over as the top team after beating Missouri 41–7 in the eighth game of the season. The following week, the Sooners topped Nebraska and Bobby Reynolds 49–35, and then beat Oklahoma State 41–14 in the regular-season finale to wrap up a perfect regular season before meeting Kentucky in the Sugar Bowl.

In 1950 UPI began a coaches poll, which would be handled by *USA Today* starting in 1991. Oklahoma was ranked No. 1 in the UPI poll as well.

The 1950 Sooners were tested often and really only blew out Big 7 opponents Missouri, Kansas, and Kansas State. The crucial win was a 14–13 nonconference defeat of Texas at the Cotton Bowl in the third game of the season. Although it was Wilkinson's third straight victory in the bitter OU-Texas series, it was his closest over UT and also demonstrated how tenuous this national title was. Oklahoma had lost most of its starters from the 1949 team, which had gone unbeaten.

"As national champions, we had tremendous morale and as much heart as I have ever seen," Wilkinson once wrote. "We were behind going into the fourth quarter in three of the 10 games [during the regular season], and yet always managed to win."

The Texas victory required a late blocked punt, setting up a touchdown by Billy Vessels and extra point by Weatherall for the one-point victory. Against Texas A&M, a 34–28 victory, the Sooners trailed 28–27 and had to depend on a rushing touchdown by Heath in the final seconds to pull it out.

"That was the game for us, " Heath said.

21 Jason White

Jason White, whose statue can be seen in Heisman Park near Memorial Stadium, claimed Oklahoma's first Heisman Trophy in a quarter of century in 2003, edging out Pittsburgh wide receiver Larry Fitzgerald by a mere 128 points. He became the first Oklahoma quarterback to win the most coveted award in college football after three OU running backs had done so.

The 6'3", 220-pound White from Tuttle, Oklahoma, never won a national title for the Sooners, losing in the BCS 1-2 game against LSU in 2003 and then again to USC in 2004. But he did battle through an injury-marred career, from 1999 through 2004, on the way to the Heisman Trophy as a junior.

Because of ligament damage in both knees that required two surgeries, White was granted an extra year to complete his eligibility. He also had back and ankle problems. Over an unusual six-year span, he completed 94 passes in his first four seasons and 533 in his last two. During his final two seasons, White was incredibly accurate on long throws in OU's stretch offense. In 2003 he set an OU record for touchdowns in a season at the time with 40. The 2003 Sooners were the highest-scoring team in Sooners history before the 2008 OU scoring juggernaut.

Jason White, the 2003 Heisman Trophy winner, stands beside a bronze statue unveiled in his honor at the Gaylord Family–Oklahoma Memorial Stadium in September 2007.

"I never thought after two surgeries that I'd be here," White told reporters at the 2003 Heisman Trophy announcement in New York City. A year later, White finished third in the Heisman Trophy voting behind his own teammate, running back Adrian Peterson, and Heisman Trophy winner Matt Leinhart of USC.

White had an obsession with chewing tobacco. Winning the Heisman Trophy wasn't as much as the focal point in New York City, but finding chewing tobacco was. He would send his handlers out to find him some chewing tobacco in the Big Apple. And it wouldn't be out of the question for White to ask his limo driver during the awards circuit to stop at a convenience store to pick some up, even in some bad neighborhoods.

White was all country. He would rather be out on the range hunting than in a tux accepting an award or standing before a bevy of microphones after a game. But he was good for Oklahoma. And he was competitive on and off the field.

He was the two-time winner of the Davey O'Brien National Quarterback Award, which is handed out at the very formal Fort Worth Club in downtown Fort Worth, Texas. It is a black-tie event, which also sponsors a scholarship award to a well-deserving high school senior.

White was rather bewildered by all the attention he received as a junior and felt he was rather ill-prepared for his acceptance speech after winning the Davey O'Brien Award. The high school senior delivered an eloquent speech. But White came back the next year and did much better, admitting he was rather embarrassed by his performance the previous year. He always made comebacks.

He was once a redshirt on the scout team. He once was a third-stringer behind Josh Heupel and then a reserve behind Nate Hybl. Finally he became a starter. Then he hit Broadway.

22 **Joe Castiglione**

Joe Castiglione had some tough first-year decisions to make as Oklahoma's athletics director.

Oklahoma football, quite frankly, was a mess after the 1998 season. Coach John Blake had suffered through three straight losing seasons. That was on top of the 5–5–1 season authored by Howard Schnellenberger in 1995. OU had gone four years without going to a bowl and had not had a league football title since 1987, a period of 11 years.

The once glorious Oklahoma football program needed refurbishing. At this point even the 65 percent winning percentage of Gary Gibbs (1989 through 1994) looked good.

Castiglione, fresh from the University of Missouri, faced perhaps Oklahoma's most important hire ever. A third straight bad football coaching hire might mean the Sooners could fall into a football abyss from which they could never escape.

So Castiglione did his homework. He didn't take the conventional route that many OU alumni wanted him to take and hire a head coach from a big program. He went the assistant-coach route and hired Bob Stoops, at the time the defensive coordinator at Florida. Two seasons later, Oklahoma had won its seventh national football title.

That was the first of a number of successful coaching hires for Castiglione, who has brought OU football back in many other areas as well in terms of fund-raising, facilities, and support staff.

Over the 16-year period heading into the 2013–14 academic year, under Castiglione's watch, the University of Oklahoma athletics department made remarkable strides:

- It increased operating revenues from $25.6 million in the fiscal year of 1998 to $100.35 million in 2013 and scholarship endowments went from $10.9 million to $3.1 million.

- It increased annual giving from $5.6 million to $21 million.
- It completed $340 million in facility construction and renovation.
- It increased both licensing and sponsorships dramatically. Licensing went up from $295,000 in 1998 to $4.1 million currently. Sponsorships increased from $2.6 million to $9 million.
- It increased football revenues from $12.4 million to $34.1 million.

In addition, Castiglione has made the right hires—coaches who have won seven national titles and more than 60 conference championships. Under Castiglione, the OU athletics department has become self-sustaining, with an $8 million surplus annually that goes to the school's academic budget. He has balanced every budget assembled during the last 16 years.

A graduate of the University of Maryland, Castiglione spent 17 years at the University of Missouri, the last five as athletics director, before becoming Oklahoma's AD.

23 Gaylord Family–Oklahoma Memorial Stadium

Football tickets for Sooners games are tough to find in Norman, Oklahoma, at any price. It's easier to go to the Oklahoma spring football game or possibly to OU's commencement to get a look inside the stadium, which has been expanded and remodeled extensively over the years.

Even with a stadium capacity of 82,112, Oklahoma averaged 84,722 for 2013 home games, and was at 103.2 percent capacity. There's a long waiting list for season tickets. Oklahoma has played in 92 consecutive sellouts going into the 2014 season—or every home game during the Bob Stoops' era, dating to the beginning of the 1999 season.

In the early part of the 2000s a $75 million expansion and renovation brought the stadium to its current seating capacity. The renovation blended the stadium into the architecture of brick and cast stone that is featured throughout the OU campus. Tree-lined plazas on the northwest, northeast, and southeast corners of the stadium, along with a clock tower and reflecting pool on the north side of the stadium, are highlights.

The stadium was renamed Gaylord Family–Oklahoma Memorial Stadium in 2002 after newspaper magnate Edward L. Gaylord and his family donated more than $50 million to the University of Oklahoma, including $22 million for a new

Coach Bob Stoops' Home Record
1999—5–0
2000—6–0
2001—6–1 (Lost to Oklahoma State 16–13)
2002—6–0
2003—7–0
2004—6–0
2005—5–1 (Lost to TCU 17–10 in season opener)
2006—6–0
2007—7–0
2008—6–0
2009—6–0
2010—6–0
2011—5–1 (Lost to Texas Tech 41–38)
2012—4–2 (Lost to Kansas State 24–19; Lost to Notre Dame 30–13)
2013—6–0

journalism building. The name Memorial, for those who died in World War I, was retained. The field continues to be named after Bennie Owen, OU's most successful early football coach, who helped raise the money for the construction of the original stadium.

The recent expansion added 8,000 seats and 27 suites in time for the 2003 season. By the following season, an additional 27 suites were added to raise the seating capacity to more than 82,000.

Heisman Park (with statues of four of the Sooners' five Heisman Trophy winners) flanks the east side of the 15th-largest stadium in the country. It offers a tour through OU history, celebrating three running backs (Billy Vessels, Steve Owens, and Billy Sims) and two quarterbacks (Jason White and Sam Bradford) who won the award.

On the north side of the stadium, Oklahoma fans can enjoy a Fan Fest starting three hours before each game. It features inflatable interactive games for children and an autograph tent with former Sooners football stars and current OU sports teams. "Go Vision"—a transportable 16 foot x 10 foot video board—shows other televised games, selected Sooners football highlights, and audience interviews.

Inside the stadium, the Pride of Oklahoma Band performs before the game, at halftime, and after the game with renditions of "Boomer Sooner" and "Oklahoma!"

Oklahoma is 87–5 at home under coach Bob Stoops from 1999 through 2013. And that record (94.5 winning percentage) has translated into the top 10 season home attendance marks in school history. Oklahoma has exceeded the home seating capacity in 57 straight games entering the 2014 season. The 86,031 who watched Notre Dame play in Norman during the 2012 season is a record attendance for a single home game.

A new video board at the south end of the stadium greeted fans at the beginning of the 2008 season. Measuring 113.5 feet wide by 32.5 feet tall (3,689 square feet), the $4.5 million board is believed to be the fourth-largest in college football. In 2008 there was also a new sound system, more ribbon boards in the upper deck, and a new Sooner Vision control room.

24 Keith Jackson

Tight end Keith Jackson grew up in Little Rock, Arkansas, where he played three sports and the cello at Parkview High School. He was also a high school honor student. But he spurned the home-state Razorbacks to head for Oklahoma and become a tight end in Barry Switzer's wishbone offense.

The 6'2", 250-pound Jackson didn't catch a lot of passes at Oklahoma, but when he did get a pass thrown his way, he knew what to do with it. He was so athletic he could dunk a basketball. And when Jackson caught a football and ran with it, he was like a tank on roller skates moving down the field. He was either too big for defensive backs to bring down or too fast for linebackers and ends to catch.

In the four seasons Jackson played at OU, from 1984 to 1987, the Sooners compiled a 42–5–1 record, won four straight Big 8 titles, went to four Orange Bowls, and won one national title (in 1985).

The two-time consensus All-American often was at his best in the big games:

- Jackson ran 88 yards on a reverse in 1985 against Nebraska, stunning the Cornhuskers and paving the way for a 27–7 victory and putting OU into the Orange Bowl. One ABC announcer remarked he had never seen a trick play work so perfectly so early in a game.

Keith Jackson speaks at the National Cowboy and Western Heritage Museum in Oklahoma City after being inducted into the Oklahoma Sports Hall of Fame in August 2006.

- In the Orange Bowl several weeks later, OU quarterback Jamelle Holieway caught Penn State in a blitz and connected with Jackson on a 71-yard touchdown pass. OU went ahead 10–7 and was on its way to a 25–10 victory over the Nittany Lions and the 1985 national title.

- In 1986 Jackson was a key player again, helping to bring Oklahoma back from a 17–10 fourth-quarter deficit against Nebraska in Lincoln. With 1:22 remaining in the game, Jackson caught a 17-yard touchdown pass from Holieway. Then, with the score tied at 17–17 and time running out, Jackson's one-handed catch past Nebraska's Broderick Thomas turned into a 41-yard gain to the Nebraska 14, setting up the winning field goal by Tim Lashar. OU won 20–17.

Had Jackson received more passes at OU, he would be in the NCAA record book as the most prolific pass-catching-for-distance tight end in major-college history. Jackson, who caught 68 passes for 1,609 yards and 15 touchdowns in his four-year college career, averaged 23.7 yards a catch with the Sooners. But he fell short of the 75-passes-caught minimum to qualify for the record. And his seasonal averages of 25.9, 27.6, and 25.2 yards-per-catch, respectively, from 1985 to 1987, would rank as the top three averages of a tight end all-time, but he didn't have the minimum 30 catches in any of those seasons.

Obviously, the NFL recognized his talent. The Philadelphia Eagles made Jackson the 13th pick in the first round of the 1988 NFL Draft, and he was the NFL offensive rookie of the year in 1988 as well. He played nine seasons in the NFL with the Eagles, Miami Dolphins, and Green Bay Packers. He played in five Pro Bowls. In later years he has worked with at-risk youths and has done sports announcing and professional speaking. He was inducted into the College Football Hall of Fame in 2001.

Jackson received the NCAA's Silver Anniversary Award, which is bestowed on "distinguished individuals on the 25th anniversary of the conclusion of their collegiate athletic careers." He became the second Oklahoma student-athlete to win the award after the late defensive tackle Lee Roy Selmon, who claimed the honor in 2001.

25 Tommy McDonald

Wiry Tommy McDonald still can leap off the ground. But in December 2008 McDonald didn't try to chest bump 6'3", 240-pound Tim Tebow, Florida's junior quarterback who won the 2008 Maxwell Award. McDonald just sort of backed away from Tebow, who looked more like a linebacker or defensive end.

For several years, the affable McDonald presented the Maxwell Award to the best player in college football on the ESPN College Football Awards Show from Lake Buena Vista, Florida. And when the quarterback looked more like a quarterback or the running back looked less like a weight-lifter, McDonald leaped into the air with a chest bump. McDonald won the Maxwell Trophy in 1956 as a senior when the Sooners were the toast of the college football world and in the midst of a 47-game winning streak.

"Tommy was a guy, he felt like every time he got that ball he ought to do something with it, make a big gain," said OU's 1953 Outland Trophy winner J.D. Roberts, who saw McDonald as a freshman.

All this bubbly behavior comes from a player who is one of the smallest, if not *the* smallest, to be inducted into the Pro Football Hall of Fame. He was inducted in 1998, 13 years after he went into the College Football Hall of Fame. McDonald was probably one of

Even in this 1956 photo, one can see Tommy McDonald's ebullient personality shine through. His annual chest bumps at the College Football Awards Show are legendary.

OU's most unlikely All-Americans, but he certainly got everything out of his 5'9", 176-pound frame. He grew up in tiny Roy, New Mexico, and somehow wound up at OU. His family moved to Albuquerque for his junior and senior seasons in 1952 and 1953, when his father moonlighted at an air base while running his own McDonald Electronics Company in Albuquerque.

"[If he hadn't made the move], I wouldn't be sitting here talking to you right now, because Roy, New Mexico, had no newspaper, no radio, no TV, no nothing," McDonald said. "Seven people graduated from that high school this past May. So the ceremony didn't last very long. Roy is about 150 miles from Albuquerque. If you blinked your eyes, you might miss it. We only had two gas stations and one supermarket. We only had 18 to 22 players on the football team."

The much bigger Highland High School in Albuquerque ran the single-wing offense, which was just made for McDonald, who had mercurial speed. He would get the ball hiked to him and he could just take off and let his natural instincts take over. "The one thing that God gave me was a big heart," McDonald said. "He made me small, but he gave me a big heart and speed.... And nothing can beat speed. You can't outrun it."

Several schools in the Southwest and Midwest recruited McDonald out of high school. But Wilkinson made the biggest impression on McDonald, who would wind up being a halfback at Oklahoma.

"I was mixed up and really didn't know where I should go," McDonald said. "Bud Wilkinson said one thing to me that really struck home. He said, 'Tommy, if you are coming here just to play football, I don't want you to come. I want you to come here to get an education, because that will last you the rest of your life.' I thought, geez, these other coaches were just worried about my four years. I didn't know what was going to happen to me after that. I thought, maybe I should go here. Lo and behold, look what happened, I went off to college and never lost a game."

Because McDonald played halfback at OU and Wilkinson usually disdained the pass, there were only glimpses of what McDonald could do catching the ball during the Sooners' heydays of the mid-1950s. Of working for his dad as an electrician his junior and senior years in high school, McDonald said, "It was a

McDonald Becomes Receiver in the NFL

Because Bud Wilkinson wanted to run the ball at Oklahoma, he only occasionally sent Tommy McDonald out as a pass receiver. But once McDonald entered professional football, the Philadelphia Eagles discovered what they had in McDonald, and he stuck at receiver the rest of his career, which spanned 12 seasons with five different teams.

"I was a halfback all this time in high school and at Oklahoma," McDonald said. "When I got to the Eagles up there, a receiver got hurt on the outside. The Eagles drafted me as a halfback. So they put me out there, and I had a 61-yard touchdown and a 25-yard touchdown. So they said, 'You are going to be a receiver from now on. You are not going to be a halfback anymore.' I cut off my sleeves then, so I could really feel the ball, when the leather hits your arms and hands."

The Oakland Raiders' star receiver Fred Biletnikoff said that during his 14-year pro career he patterned himself after McDonald with his own cut-off sleeves. "I just thought he was saying that," McDonald said. "But he did, he really did."

blessing in disguise because working for him those two years, it made my wrists very, very strong when I would catch the ball. With me working with a screwdriver and doing a lot of outlets in houses, it made my fingers really strong. I used to shake hands with people, and they would say, 'You have a good grip.'"

His senior year against Texas in a 45–0 victory, McDonald made a long touchdown catch, one of the times Wilkinson let him loose. In the film sessions later, Wilkinson remarked to him, "I don't know how you caught that ball, Tommy." McDonald said, "That's what Wilkinson told me. I caught the last rear end part of the ball. I didn't catch the middle of it. I didn't catch the front of it."

Drafted in the third round of the 1957 NFL Draft by the Philadelphia Eagles, McDonald also completed 29 of 48 passes at OU to go along with nearly 1,700 yards rushing. In 1955 he became the first Sooner to score a touchdown in every game during a season.

"I thank God for that kind of attitude that he gave me [always thinking he could make a big play]," McDonald said. "When I stepped across the white line onto the field, it was strictly business. It was not play anymore."

26 Bedlam

For more than 100 years, Oklahoma has owned the upper hand in the Bedlam Series with Oklahoma State. The Sooners, through the 2013 season, owned an 84–17–7 advantage in a rivalry that started in 1904 in Guthrie, Oklahoma.

The Sooners won that game 75–0, a little less than three years before Oklahoma even became a state, in 1907. That lopsided OU victory set the tone for the rest of the century. Oklahoma State (formerly Oklahoma A&M) didn't even score in the first eight games that rotated between Stillwater and Norman. The Cowboys finally broke through with a score in the ninth game and lost 28–6.

In 1917 Oklahoma State won its first game against OU, 9–0 in Oklahoma City. But by that time, the Cowboys were down in the series 1–11. And they have never been able to catch up to their big brother Sooners.

So why Bedlam? The first game was on a bitterly cold and very windy day. When Oklahoma A&M punted once, the ball went backward, down a hill, and into the icy waters of a creek. If Oklahoma recovered, it would be a touchdown. So players from both teams dove into the water. OU got the ball for a score and has led ever since. It's been a hard-hitting game through the years for good reason.

Other Notable Escapes, Mostly Against Nebraska

November 22, 1980: Oklahoma 21, Nebraska 17 in Lincoln
Buster Rhymes scored the game-winner from the 1-yard line with less than a minute remaining. He also had a 43-yard run to the 16-yard line during the last-gasp drive. Nebraska quarterback Jeff Quinn also scored from the 1-yard line with 3:16 left to give Nebraska the lead. But Oklahoma prevailed to win the Big 8 title and Orange Bowl berth.

January 1, 1981: Oklahoma 18, Florida State 17 at the Orange Bowl
Oklahoma lost four fumbles. But a 78-yard drive led by quarterback J.C. Watts, including a 42-yard pass to Steve Rhodes on third-and-nine provided Sooner Magic. Watts passed 11 yards to Rhodes for a touchdown with 1:27 remaining. A two-point conversion pass to tight end Forrest Valora provided the winning points.

November 17, 1984: Oklahoma 17, Nebraska 7 in Lincoln
Nebraska was the No. 1 team in the country. But OU Tim Lashar's 32-yard field goal early in the fourth quarter gave OU a 10–7 lead. Oklahoma stopped Nebraska I-back Jeff Smith on fourth-and-one at the OU 1 in the fourth quarter. Then OU quarterback Danny Bradley scored on a 29-yard run with just under a minute to play to ensure the victory.

November 22, 1986: Oklahoma 20, Nebraska 17 in Lincoln
OU quarterback Jamelle Holieway led a comeback from 17–10 with 4:10 left. The game appeared to be over when Holieway fumbled on fourth down at the OU 15. But a face-mask penalty gave the Sooners new life. Keith Jackson caught an 18-yard touchdown pass to tie the game. Then Jackson's one-handed catch past Nebraska's Broderick Thomas turned into a 41-yard gain, setting up the winning field goal by Tim Lashar.

"There's nothing more humiliating to an OU player than Oklahoma State coming into your hometown and whipping you," said Oklahoma radio-television personality and former Sooners quarterback Dean Blevins. He suffered that very fate, 31–24 in 1976. "OU players would prefer to lose to Nebraska or Texas," he said.

OU fans tend to make fun of that Aggie School up I-35 in the red clay country.

Pat Quinn, a former sports information director at Oklahoma State, one time was preparing to address a group, and an OU fan, knowing who he was, asked, "Is it true the Oklahoma State homecoming queen grazes at halftime?" Quinn darted back honestly, "Sir, I will have you know you are talking about my daughter."

Through the 2013 season the Sooners have won 10 of the last 11 football games against Oklahoma State, including a 33–24 decision this past season that vaulted OU into the Sugar Bowl and knocked Oklahoma State out of a tie for the Big 12 title and a berth in the Fiesta Bowl. But before the current 10-of-11 string OSU had won five of the previous eight against the Sooners.

Oklahoma coach Bob Stoops has lost only five home games during his 15-year tenure in Norman. But one of those was a bitter 16–13 defeat to 27-point underdog Oklahoma State in 2001. Late in the season, the fourth-ranked Sooners were knocked out of a slot in the Big 12 title game and chance to play for a second straight national championship. OSU's Josh Fields hit Rashaun Woods on a 14-yard touchdown pass with 1:36 remaining to beat the Sooners.

In 2002 Oklahoma State beat Oklahoma again, 38–28 in Stillwater. The Sooners still won the Big 12 title. But it was OU's second loss of the season and it knocked them out of any chance of the national title. OU wound up going to the Rose Bowl and beating Washington State.

Historically, the football games have meant Oklahoma State heartbreak or lopsided losses to OU. After an OSU victory in 1976, the Cowboys didn't win again until 1995 in Howard Schnellenberger's only season as the Sooners' coach.

There's a formula for the OU-OSU series for all men's and women's sports—wrestling, baseball, basketball, etc. And the school with the most points at the end of a school year wins the series. But football is the main focus of the bragging rights.

27 Sooner Magic

The birthplace of "Sooner Magic" occurred in a 1976 Oklahoma-Nebraska game in Lincoln when Oklahoma pulled out a pulsating 20–17 win. Reserve quarterback Dean Blevins was a central figure in the 1976 game.

"It was the first thing that developed the magic, us being the underdogs and us still winning," said Blevins. "We had won two championships in 1974 and 1975. We were down a little bit. We went to Nebraska, and they had Vince Ferragamo at quarterback and a lot of big names. They were good, better than us. It was a cold, blustery day, and Nebraska had the lead late in the game. I didn't come in 'til the very end of the game."

Oklahoma trailed 17–13 with 85 yards to score. So Switzer emptied his playbook. And the Sooners needed a quarterback in the game who could pass. A halfback option pass from sophomore Woodie Shepard to split end Steve Rhodes covered 47 yards. But it came down to a third-and-20 at the Cornhuskers' 34 with 44 seconds to go for the play of the game. Ah, Sooner Magic.

"It was one of those real clutch situations going into wind, the most miserable conditions," Blevins said. "The play was called 'Left 3-17, stop, and lateral.' We had run it so many times in practice. I would look out and see coverage in secondary. They had busted coverage. It was the only time they busted all day. They did it on one play."

Blevins entered the game because he was a good passer. He threw a strike to Rhodes, who was split left. He caught it 10 yards downfield and lateraled to halfback Elvis Peacock, who caught it in a full gallop. The Nebraska defenders went to tackle Rhodes, but Peacock, with a 9.4-second speed in the 100, took it down to the

Nebraska 2-yard line before he was bumped out of bounds. On the next play, Peacock scored. And Oklahoma had a highly unlikely 20–17 victory.

28 Greg Pruitt

Perhaps there has never been a more flamboyant and versatile player to put on a Sooners uniform. Hailing from Houston, Texas, the 5'9", 177-pound Greg Pruitt electrified fans with his rushing, receiving, and punt and kickoff returning in the early 1970s.

He was a key cog as a halfback in OU's then-new ground-guzzling wishbone offense when he was named a consensus All-American during the 1971 and 1972 seasons. He probably took a backseat only to Nebraska's Johnny Rodgers, whose team won the national title in 1971 by beating OU and who won the 1972 Heisman Trophy.

"Nebraska was more four yards and a cloud of dust, with big, ol' physical linemen," said Jim Dickey, an OU defensive assistant coach from 1969 to 1972. "I'd say with Joe Wylie [another halfback in that era] and Greg Pruitt, we had some flashy guys. We tried to tackle him [Pruitt] in the spring and we couldn't. He had this burst. We always timed the 40-yard dash. And he could get started as fast as anyone I have ever seen."

During his three-year varsity career at OU, Pruitt will be remembered as putting the zip in the wishbone and helping restore the Sooners to national prominence in 1971 after three straight four-loss seasons. He still ranks third among Sooners in career all-purpose yards. Pruitt gained 3,122 rushing yards, 491 receiving yards, 139 yards on punt returns, and 679 yards returning kickoffs. And he scored 41 career touchdowns as a Sooner.

In 1970 Oklahoma coach Chuck Fairbanks switched to the wishbone offense in a 41–9 loss to Texas. But by the end of the season, OU and Pruitt started to hit their stride with the triple-option offense. In a 24–24 tie with Alabama in Pruitt's hometown 1970 Bluebonnet Bowl, Pruitt had touchdown runs of 58 and 25 yards and was named one of the bowl's MVPs as only a sophomore.

Then, as a junior, he rushed for 1,760 yards, including three 200-yard plus games. His 294 yards rushing in a 75–28 victory over Kansas State is still an OU individual game record, as is his all- purpose yards total of 374 in that game. Oklahoma led the nation in rushing yards per game with a still-record 472.4 a game, although it did lose the Game of the Century to Nebraska 35–31, and wound up 11–1. Pruitt averaged an incredible nine yards a rush as a junior and finished third in the Heisman Trophy balloting that season behind Auburn quarterback Pat Sullivan and Cornell running back Ed Marinaro.

As a senior, Pruitt was expected to contend for the Heisman Trophy but suffered a twisted ankle against Kansas in the ninth game of the season. The next week, neither he nor Rodgers, who ultimately would beat out Pruitt for the Heisman Trophy, were much of a factor in OU's 17–14 victory over Nebraska. The two teams tied for the Big 12 title, but Nebraska went to the Orange Bowl, and OU to the Sugar Bowl a second straight season.

"Pruitt got real mad at the Sugar Bowl when he didn't win the Heisman Trophy," Dickey said. "He didn't ride with the team to the game. Chuck was not going to let him play. Barry [Switzer] didn't think that was real smart. That would punish us. Chuck went a long way to getting Barry the head job. But Barry wasn't a yes man—he told him what he thought. Sometimes Chuck would go with him and sometimes he would go the other way. We had left Pruitt at the hotel. They brought him to the stadium and debated whether to let him play or not. He played, and we barely beat Penn State 14–0."

Pruitt was drafted in the second round by the Cleveland Browns and played 12 seasons in the National Football League with the Browns and the Los Angeles Raiders. He was selected to five Pro Bowls and was later inducted into the College Football Hall of Fame in 1999.

29 Stoops' Record

On November 23, 2013, Bob Stoops passed Barry Switzer as the all-time winningest coach in Oklahoma football history. He's No. 1 at OU in coaching victories with 160 entering the 2014 season— that's an average of more than 10 wins a season playing one of the toughest schedules in college football.

Stoops' 15-year run at Oklahoma (since the 1999 season) also includes more Bowl Championship Series appearances (nine) than any other coach in college football. He wound up 4–5 in those games, after winning his last two BCS Bowls.

Stoops has the distinction of being the only college coach to win all four BCS Bowls (Fiesta, Rose, Sugar, Orange) and the national championship during the era that closed following games in January 2014.

"Bobby and Barry are out of the same mold," said former Iowa coach Hayden Fry, under whom Stoops was an assistant coach. "They are winners. They are great men to play for…The coaching bloodline is in the [Stoops] family. I never hired an assistant coach in my life, in 47 years of coaching, unless I was completely convinced that he was motivated to become a head coach."

Stoops' BCS Record

2000: BCS Championship Game (Orange Bowl): **Oklahoma** 13,
 Florida State 2
2002: Rose Bowl: **Oklahoma** 34, Washington State 14
2003: BCS Championship Game (Sugar Bowl): LSU 21, **Oklahoma** 14
2004: BCS Championship Game (Orange Bowl): USC 55,
 Oklahoma 19
2006: Fiesta Bowl: Boise State 43, **Oklahoma** 42 (OT)
2007: Fiesta Bowl: West Virginia 48, **Oklahoma** 28
2008: BCS Championship Game (Orange Bowl): Florida 24,
 Oklahoma 14
2010: Fiesta Bowl: **Oklahoma** 48, Connecticut 20
2013: Sugar Bowl: **Oklahoma** 45, Alabama 31

From Stoops' second season in 2000, Oklahoma leads BCS Conferences in several categories, including: victories (153), winning percentage (81.8), regular-season conference victories (94), regular-season conference winning percentage (81.7), total touchdowns (881), turnover differential (+108), and takeaways (410).

"I don't remember what game I passed Bud Wilkinson years ago...." Switzer said of the previous OU coaching giant. "But it is a big deal to be the winningest coach in the history of Oklahoma football, because the history of Oklahoma football casts a long shadow over the entire game of college football."

30 Oklahoma-Nebraska Series

It used to be *the* series in the Midlands. Now, the teams aren't even in the same conference after Nebraska's departure from the Big 12 Conference to the Big Ten in 2011.

Starting in the early 1960s and continuing for more than 25 years, the Oklahoma-Nebraska game had both national and regional significance. The two Big Reds dominated the old Big 8 Conference, and the game was on some kind of television network or cable almost every year, usually late in the season.

NU-OU became a Thanksgiving weekend staple, as much as turkey and dressing and early Christmas shopping. Coaching names such as Bob Devaney, Tom Osborne, Chuck Fairbanks, and Barry Switzer made impressions on television viewers everywhere. Players such as Johnny Rodgers, Greg Pruitt, Billy Sims, and Jerry Tagge became household names because of the unique exposure.

From 1962 to 1988, Oklahoma won or tied for the Big 8 title 15 times, and Nebraska won or tied for it 15 times. No other team in the league won the title outright without one of the two Big Reds getting at least a share of it. That is how dominant the teams in Norman and Lincoln were.

But with the formation of the Big 12 Conference in 1996, Nebraska was competing in the North Division of the league and Oklahoma was in the South. Because of the rotation of opponents in crossover games between divisions, it meant there would be two-year gaps in regularly scheduled games between the two Big Reds. That was unless the teams scheduled a nonconference game in the two-year period when they weren't playing conference games.

Nebraska and Oklahoma played 71 straight seasons, from 1927 through 1997. Then in 1998 the streak stopped.

"We wanted to play it every year, even on a nonconference basis," said Bill Byrne, Nebraska's athletics director at the time. "And we made that offer to Oklahoma. And they weren't quite as interested as we were. They told us their rival was the University of Texas."

Oklahoma officials took a different approach to scheduling nonconference games, considering the tougher nature of having to face teams such as Texas Tech and Texas A&M every year, along

Youngsters from a nearby boys camp get a thrill chatting with Heisman Trophy winner Steve Owens of Oklahoma in July 1970 as the college all-stars suited up for practice at Northwestern University's Dyche Stadium in Evanston, Illinois. The college gridders played the reigning pro champion Kansas City Chiefs in the annual All-Star Game at Chicago's Soldier Field.

with Texas, in the South Division. The Sooners usually play one name opponent during the nonconference portion of their schedule. Adding a rivalry game like Nebraska didn't fit.

"The reality is they weren't our chief rival," said Donnie Duncan, who was OU's athletics director at the time of the formation of the Big 12. "And they still aren't. Texas is.... I couldn't think of any really good reasons why we *should* renew the rivalry on an every-year basis. We were still going to be playing two out of every four years. And we were playing teams at the time the caliber of USC and UCLA, teams you recruit to, places where there might be players.... And trips to the East like Pittsburgh or maybe the University of Miami."

Duncan added he never got one letter from a fan about not playing Nebraska on an every-year basis.

In 2008, on the eve of Oklahoma's 62–28 victory over the Cornhuskers in Norman, Oklahoma athletics director Joe Castiglione organized a reunion of players and coaches on both sides who have played in the 1971 Game of the Century, won by Nebraska 35–31. It was an effort to celebrate the series, which Oklahoma now leads 45–38–3.

In 2004 and 2005 problems occurred between the two football programs.

A Nebraska player, lineman Darren DeLone collided with one of the Oklahoma RUF/NEKS, Adam Merritt, during pregame warmups in 2004 in Norman, causing the Oklahoma fan injuries. Merritt filed a lawsuit, but DeLone was later acquitted. After that game, a 30–3 OU victory, Nebraska coach Bill Callahan called OU fans "hillbillies." In 2005 Callahan made a throat- slashing gesture toward a Big 12 official during Oklahoma's 31–24 victory over the Cornhuskers in Lincoln. He was later reprimanded by the league office.

Oklahoma had a 6–4 record against Nebraska in the Big 12 Conference, including two victories over the Cornhuskers in Big 12 title games (2006 and 2010). The two teams are scheduled to renew their rivalry on September 18, 2021, in Norman with a return game in Lincoln the following season. The 2021 game would coincide with the 50th anniversary of the Game of the Century.

Nebraska-Oklahoma's Big 8 Domination
From 1962 to 1988, Oklahoma and/or Nebraska had at least a piece of the title every year.

Year	Champion	Coach
1962	Oklahoma (7–0)	Bud Wilkinson
1963	Nebraska (7–0)	Bob Devaney
1964	Nebraska (6–1)	Bob Devaney
1965	Nebraska (7–0)	Bob Devaney
1966	Nebraska (6–1)	Bob Devaney
1967	Oklahoma (7–0)	Chuck Fairbanks
1968	Oklahoma/Kansas (6–1)	Chuck Fairbanks/Pepper Rodgers
1969	Nebraska/Missouri (6–1)	Bob Devaney/Dan Devine
1970	Nebraska (7–0)	Bob Devaney
1971	Nebraska (7–0)	Bob Devaney
1972	Nebraska (5–1–1)	Bob Devaney
1973	Oklahoma (7–0)	Barry Switzer
1974	Oklahoma (7–0)	Barry Switzer
1975	Nebraska/Oklahoma (6–1)	Tom Osborne/Barry Switzer
1976	Colorado/Oklahoma/ Oklahoma St. (5–2)	Bill Mallory/Barry Switzer/ Jim Stanley
1977	Oklahoma (7–0)	Barry Switzer
1978	Nebraska/Oklahoma (6–1)	Tom Osborne/Barry Switzer
1979	Oklahoma (7–0)	Barry Switzer
1980	Oklahoma (7–0)	Barry Switzer
1981	Nebraska(7–0)	Tom Osborne
1982	Nebraska(7–0)	Tom Osborne
1983	Nebraska(7–0)	Tom Osborne
1984	Oklahoma/Nebraska (6–1)	Barry Switzer/Tom Osborne
1985	Oklahoma (7–0)	Barry Switzer
1986	Oklahoma (7–0)	Barry Switzer
1987	Oklahoma (7–0)	Barry Switzer
1988	Nebraska (7–0)	Tom Osborne

31 Steve Owens

Owens was not known as much for a fancy style of running, but for his brutal effectiveness. In 1969, playing on an average 6–4 Oklahoma team, Owens was a human battering ram against opposing defensive lines.

By the time he was finished, he rushed for 57 career touchdowns, an NCAA record at the time for a three-year player (1967–1969). And many of these were on short plunges after he carried the Sooners on his back down the field. Twice in his career, Owens carried the ball more than 50 times in a game during a Sooners era when he was much of the pre-wishbone offense. As a senior in 1969, he became Oklahoma's second Heisman Trophy winner when he led the country in rushing (1,523 yards) and scoring (138 points).

"One of the things I do remember is we were playing them in a National ABC game, and we were beating them pretty bad," said Missouri defensive back Dennis Poppe. "He had a continuous streak of 100-yard games. I remember him just getting the ball.... He didn't look like a fast running back. I found out tackling him that he was the real thing."

In a 44–10 loss to Missouri in Columbia, Owens carried the ball 29 times, as the Tigers were on their way to a share of the Big 8 championship with Nebraska.

From the second game of the 1968 season (Owens' junior season) through the eighth game of his senior season, Owens rushed for 100 or more yards in 17 straight regular-season games and for more than 100 yards in a 1968 Bluebonnet Bowl loss to SMU for a total of 18 straight games.

Steve Owens' Streak of 100-Yard Games

1968

Opponent	Carries	Yards
North Carolina State	37	164
Texas	30	127
Iowa State	36	175
Colorado	33	193
Kansas State	47	185
Kansas	37	157
Missouri	46	177
Nebraska	41	172
Oklahoma State	34	120
SMU	36	113

1969

Wisconsin	40	189
Pittsburgh	29	104
Texas	30	123
Colorado	28	112
Kansas State	29	105
Iowa State	53	248
Missouri	29	109
Kansas	44	201

His 100-yard rushing streak ended in a 44–14 loss to Nebraska in 1969. But Owens saved his best for last in his final game as a Sooner in the 1969 season finale. He rushed a personal-high 55 times for a personal-best 261 yards in a 28–27 victory over Oklahoma State.

One interesting footnote to Owens' career is that he rushed for more than 100 yards each time the Sooners played Texas, but he never came away with a victory over the hated Longhorns.

Even more than 40 years later, Owens is not an afterthought. A first-round draft choice, he played for the Detroit Lions in the 1970s before a knee injury ended his career. Much later he served as OU's athletics director, from 1996 to 1998. He still holds OU records for rushing attempts in a game (55), in a season (393 in 1968), and in a career (958). Through 2013, he ranked fourth all-time in career rushing yards at OU, with 4,041 yards.

32 Jim Weatherall

Oklahoma's standout tackle Jim Weatherall, the school's first Outland Trophy winner in 1951, was a mountain of a man. He towered over teammates even on Bud Wilkinson's powerhouse teams.

"Weatherall, probably out of my years there, was the best lineman we had," said 1953 Outland Trophy winner J.D. Roberts. "He was a pretty good-sized guy at that time. He was strong. He was a very good player offensively and defensively. He and Lee Roy Selmon [the 1975 Outland Trophy winner] were probably the two best that we had.... I was a lot different player from Jim. Jim was a big guy. I was short and stocky."

Weatherall, 6'4", 230 pounds, lived on a ranch in West Texas and played football at White Deer High School after previously living in Norman. He was the strong, silent type, remembers the late Eddie Crowder, an OU teammate during the era: "He seemed mammoth to us." Weatherall was also a heavyweight wrestler two seasons for the Sooners.

In that era, before weight-lifting had taken hold in college football, linemen his size weren't athletic; they usually were fat. But Weatherall had very little body fat and was athletic. He was noticed as a freshman in 1948, and by spring practice before the 1949 season, he had taken hold. He not only played tackle on both

Oklahoma's Outland Trophy Winners

1951–Jim Weatherall, Tackle, 6'4", 230, Played NFL—Philly, Washington, Detroit (six seasons total)

1953–J.D. Roberts, Guard, 5'10", 210, Played NFL—Drafted by Green Bay, later head coach of the New Orleans Saints (1970–1972)

1975–Lee Roy Selmon, Defensive Tackle, 6'2", 256, Played NFL—Tampa Bay (nine seasons)

1978–Greg Roberts, Offensive Guard, 6'3", 240, Played NFL—Tampa Bay (four seasons)

2004–Jammal Brown, Offensive Tackle, 6'6", 313, Played NFL—New Orleans (2005–2009), Washington Redskins (2010–11)

sides of the ball, he also kicked off for the Sooners and kicked extra points.

Although the Sooners did not kick field goals in those days, Weatherall was still busy as a place-kicker because of OU's prolific offense. In 1950 he was fifth in the nation in scoring among place-kickers and in 1951 he was second.

As a sophomore in 1949, Weatherall was an anchor on an OU team that went 11–0 and blasted Louisiana State 35–0 in the Sugar Bowl. The following season the Sooners won the first of three national titles under Wilkinson, and Weatherall's place-kicking—including an extra point in a 14–13 victory over Texas—proved crucial in the national title drive.

During his junior and senior seasons, Weatherall was a consensus All-American for the Sooners, who had won 31 straight games from 1948 to 1950, finally falling to Kentucky in the Sugar Bowl on January 1, 1951.

Although the 1951 Sooners lost two of their first three games against Texas A&M (14–7) and Texas (9–7), Weatherall won the Outland Trophy in his senior season. The Sooners won their final seven games and another Big 7 Conference championship.

Weatherall was most noted for his defensive prowess. And the 1951 team won with defense, holding six opponents to less than 10 points.

Weatherall played professional football and later opened a oil-business-related mud-drilling company in Oklahoma City. He died while playing racquet ball in 1992, the same year he was inducted into the College Football Hall of Fame.

33 Staying in the Big 12

Oklahoma faced a confusing crossroads in 2010 and 2011 as the Big 12 Conference fought for its very existence.

In early June of 2010, OU's longtime Big Eight rival Nebraska announced it would join the Big Ten Conference. About the same time, Colorado revealed it would head west to join the Pacific 10 Conference.

That left the Big 12 with 10 teams, two fewer than what was needed for two six-team divisions that the NCAA mandates for playing a football title game.

Pac 10 commissioner Larry Scott, after landing Colorado, then made a bold move. He offered the Sooners a move west to possibly form the Pacific 16 Conference, along with Oklahoma State, Texas, and Texas Tech. Scott even got on a plane and visited those campuses, unveiling scheduling matrixes and the offer of a lucrative cable network deal.

Oddly enough, Oklahoma and Texas were the key players in keeping the Big 12 afloat. In the end, addition by subtraction of Colorado and Nebraska meant 10 Big 12 schools could divide money better than 12.

Behind the scenes, the two schools worked with then commissioner Dan Beebe to reboot the Big 12. One major snag for OU helping to form the Pac-16 was the fact Texas had plans for its own cable network (ultimately ESPN's Longhorn Network) and wouldn't give up its cable rights. That was the deal breaker with Scott.

OU athletic director Joe Castiglione and then Texas athletic director Deloss Dodds met at Bob's Steak and Chophouse on Lemmon Avenue in Dallas, sitting in a booth in plain view of patrons to hammer out "a new Big 12." It worked.

So for a season, everything looked fine.

Then in the summer of 2011 Texas' Longhorn Network came into being. Texas A&M got antsy and alarmed about UT's aggressiveness and believed the network would give the Longhorns an upper hand in recruiting. The Aggies resumed talks with the Southeastern Conference. Missouri, too, had concerns about the Longhorn Network and comments by Oklahoma president David Boren that the Sooners would consider moving to the Pac 12 in light of A&M's overtures to the SEC. Missouri's talks with the SEC intensified. A&M and Missouri eventually announced they would leave the Big 12 for the SEC in 2012.

Meanwhile, the Pac 12's Scott made another run at Texas, Oklahoma, and the other Big 12 schools. But the remaining eight Big 12 schools, including Oklahoma, wound up agreeing to grant their first- and second-tier media rights to the conference for a period of six years, allowing UT to continue with is network. The Big 12 invited TCU and West Virginia to replace Texas A&M and Missouri, respectively, and settled in with just 10 teams again.

34 1971 Sooners

They won nine straight games before a 35–31 loss to Nebraska in the Game of the Century cost them the national title in game No. 10. They scored 75 points in one game against Kansas State. They had one of their best quarterbacks ever, Jack Mildren.

"I have always said the greatest team not to win a national championship was the 1971 Oklahoma team," said Jim Walden, who was a Nebraska assistant coach in 1971. "It would have been a champion any other year. I have always said it was the most deserved team that didn't win the championship."

The offense was simply mind-boggling on the ground. The Sooners' wishbone gobbled up a still–NCAA record 472.4 rushing yards a game. Oklahoma led the country in total offense with 566.5 yards a game. And the Sooners were the highest scoring team in the country with 44.9 points a game.

The 1971 Sooners finished second in the Associated Press poll behind Nebraska and third in the coaches poll behind Nebraska and Alabama. Following the loss to Nebraska, the Sooners rocked Oklahoma State 58–14 in the regular-season finale and then beat Auburn in the Sugar Bowl. Nebraska humbled Alabama 38–6 in the Orange Bowl. Oklahoma obviously would have been No. 2 in the coaches' poll as well if it had been taken after the bowls.

The 1971 OU team had nine All–Big 8 players on its roster:

Tight end Al Chandler: In the wishbone, Chandler didn't get the opportunity to catch a lot of passes, but he played six seasons in the NFL for three different teams: Cincinnati, New England, and St. Louis.

Offensive guard Ken Jones: Jones was the second-best offensive lineman behind Brahaney. He later played some at center.

Center Tom Brahaney: Brahaney was a College Football Hall of Famer. Nebraska's Rich Glover called him the best center he ever played against after the Game of the Century. Brahaney played nine seasons with the St. Louis Football Cardinals.

Quarterback Jack Mildren: Mildren beat the 1971 Heisman Trophy winner, Auburn's Pat Sullivan, in a head-to-head matchup, 40–22, in the Sugar Bowl to put an exclamation mark on a sterling OU career. As a dual running-passing threat, he finished his three-year OU career with 5,117 yards in total offense.

Running back Greg Pruitt: One of three All-Americans on the team, along with Mildren and Brahaney, Pruitt averaged 9.0 yards per carry and rushed for 18 touchdowns and 1,760 yards as a junior. He finished third in the Heisman Trophy balloting in 1971 and later had a long and successful career with the Cleveland Browns and the Los Angeles Raiders.

Defensive lineman Raymond Hamilton: Hamilton led the Sooners with four fumble recoveries in 1971 and the next season in tackles for loss. He wound up playing nine seasons for the New England Patriots.

Defensive tackle Derland Moore: A big-play specialist who would be All-America as a senior in 1972, Moore, a former walk-on at OU, played 13 seasons with the New Orleans Saints and one season with the New York Jets in 1986.

Linebacker Steve Aycock: A steady player who was a two-time All-Conference player, Aycock led the Sooners with 175 total tackles as a junior in 1970.

Defensive back John Shelley: A senior in 1971, Shelley led the Sooners with five interceptions and 14 pass deflections.

35 Cleaning Up After Barry

Former Sooners football player Gary Gibbs, a loyal assistant to Barry Switzer for 14 years as defensive coordinator/linebackers coach, took over the tarnished Oklahoma program in the summer of 1989. The Sooners faced NCAA probation, with a one-year television ban, a two-year bowl ban, and scholarship and recruiting-visit reductions. Oklahoma also had to endure the lasting impressions of law-breaking transgressions of several football players under Switzer.

Bud Wilkinson Hall, the football players' on-campus dormitory, had become a hall of horrors for those living there and hardly honored its namesake. One teammate shot another with a .22–caliber revolver, two others were alleged to have raped an Oklahoma City woman. And OU's starting quarterback, Charles Thompson, had been arrested on a cocaine charge, was convicted, and later ended up in federal prison in Big Spring, Texas. He later coauthored a book while in prison and then returned at 24 to play football at Central State (Ohio) as a running back.

By fall 1989 those players were all out of the program, and several others had either left or were dismissed by Gibbs, who tightened the reins. Recruiting had suffered. The image of the OU program was at an all-time low. Heading into the 1989 season, Oklahoma was down to 77 total players on scholarship (95 is the limit).

"We all know we are living in a glass house now," Gibbs said in a 1989 interview. "But we are Oklahoma. People always look to us. We have too many people [to be down].… We can't let the actions of five people distort the great program here at the University of Oklahoma."

Oklahoma athletics director Donnie Duncan had hired former NCAA investigator Ron Watson as compliance director and Thomas

The Barry and Bob Show

The winner of the 1980 Oklahoma-Nebraska game in Lincoln would win the Big 8 championship and go to the Orange Bowl. The loser would go to the Sun Bowl in El Paso. So Oklahoma coach Barry Switzer lightened up the pregame festivities.

Bob Devaney, then–Nebraska athletics director, was taping his show on the Friday before the game. He was holding a pineapple and crowing about how the Sooners would have to eat tamales in El Paso. On the show, Switzer snuck up on the set behind him and handed him a bag of tacos from Taco Bell.

After a 21–17 Oklahoma victory, Switzer asked on television, "Are there any good Mexican restaurants in Miami?" He was eating an orange. Oklahoma went on to beat Florida State 18–17 in the Orange Bowl. Nebraska beat Mississippi State 31–17 in the Sun Bowl.

Hill as academic counselor to lead OU out of the wilderness. But he added that OU also had to focus on the right kind of kids.

Gibbs enforced a strict team dress code. Players needed to cut their hair and lose the earrings—at least in public settings. Gibbs also had two members of the football support staff live in Bud Wilkinson Hall to help monitor the players' behavior.

Unlike the flashy and outspoken Switzer, Gibbs was a 180-degree difference. When he showed up at his first practice, he was hardly noticeable on the field, unlike Switzer who usually was the center of attention. And when he did speak, he was speaking in coach-speak, not in the juicy quotes "the King" would usually hand out. "He's not going to be in the public eye, like Barry was," said one of his staff members. And he wasn't.

"He was a 180, but a strong 180," Duncan said of Gibbs, who moved into Switzer's head spot. "Gary took over when it was a perilous time. Barry resigned on June 19. And we were on a two-year probation and a two-year bowl ban. And that meant any of our juniors or seniors who were precluded from going to a bowl could have transferred and played immediately."

Duncan said a mass exodus was possible if a coach on the current staff hadn't been hired as Switzer's replacement and kept connections with assistants, players, and future recruits. He said the defection of players could have been so catastrophic, the program might not have recovered for 14 years, numbers-wise. "And that's after going everywhere and getting beat like a junior varsity team," Duncan said.

Duncan said Gibbs was the man to restore the image because "he ran off enough football players to win a lot of football games." And he was adamant in a team meeting when Switzer was still the head coach of ridding the program of problem players.

Gibbs' worst failings were the facts he was a) following a legend in Switzer, albeit tarnished, but still revered by many, and b) unable to beat Texas (1–5). Switzer won 83.7 percent of his games and 12 Big 8 titles—which gave him cover for his problems at the end. Gibbs white-washed the program but won only 65.2 percent of his games and zero Big 8 championships.

"I understand when you don't win, that is part of the business," Duncan said. "But for knowing what I know, if he hadn't been the man he was and done the job he did, Oklahoma's program would have been very different today. So as you can tell, I have the highest regard for Gary as a person and as a coach."

36 Roy Williams

On the front of the October 15, 2001, issue of *Sports Illustrated*, you'll see the Sooners' Jimmy Wilkerson crushing UT quarterback Chris Simms during a 14–3 Oklahoma victory the previous Saturday at the Cotton Bowl in Dallas. Purchase a reprint. It is a keepsake, Sooners fans.

The cover doesn't have the play of the century perhaps, which had OU's strong safety Roy Williams leaping in the air—"It's a bird, it's a plane, no it is Super-Roy"—making the play that preserved defending national champion Oklahoma's 18th straight victory. But it is representative of what the game was all about—hard-hitting, nasty defense by the Sooners, who made Simms' life miserable the entire game.

The flying motion that earned Williams the nickname Superman had been discouraged by OU defensive coordinator Mike Stoops. "Coach had told me before not to jump," Williams said. "When I did it before, I left a gap open."

With about two minutes remaining in the game, Oklahoma led 7–3. And the Sooners had the Longhorns backed up on their own 3-yard line after a pooch punt had pinned them there. Williams came on a blitz, left his feet, leaping over a blocking back and hitting Simms' throwing arm. The ball was deflected into the waiting arms of OU's sophomore linebacker Teddy Lehman, who basically could walk into the end zone for the clinching touchdown of a 14–3 victory.

"There is no doubt that he is the most productive and active defensive back I have coached or have ever been around as far as impacting a game, making big plays, and producing turnovers," said Oklahoma coach Bob Stoops of Williams. "And he's the best open-field tackler I have ever seen."

Williams followed that defensive play with an interception of Simms as the game wound down. The Superman play is just part of Williams' highlight reel during the 2001 season, when he won both the Bronko Nagurski (best defensive player in the nation) and Jim Thorpe (best defensive back in the nation) Awards.

The 2001 Big 12 Defensive Player of the Year put up gargantuan numbers defensively during that regular season: 14 tackles for loss (-57 yards), five interceptions, 22 passes broken up, three fumble recoveries (one of which he returned for a touchdown), and 101 tackles (73 unassisted).

As a result, the 6', 220-pound Williams elected to bypass his senior season at Oklahoma and was selected eighth overall by the Dallas Cowboys in the 2002 NFL Draft. He was named to the Pro Bowl five times as a Cowboy during his seven-year career in Dallas. He retired following the 2010 season after spending two seasons in Cincinnati.

The historic play in the 2001 Oklahoma-Texas game has been depicted on a mural plaque, which is located in the Roy Williams Strength and Speed Complex on the University of Oklahoma campus. Williams contributed to the construction of the facility, which also honors his athletic achievements.

37 *Oklahoma!*

Oklahoma's emergence as a national football power in the late 1940s occurred a few years after the hit Broadway musical *Oklahoma!* first opened on March 31, 1943, at the St. James Theatre in New York City. *Oklahoma!* has been one of the most successful musicals of all-time and at the time served as an energizing force for a state, a school, and a football team.

DVDs of the movie are available everywhere, and the musical is often revived on stage at major theaters and is a popular choice for high school, college, and community productions.

Depicting much of Oklahoma life in the early 1900s, when Oklahoma would become a state (1907), *Oklahoma!* was one of the first "book musicals," in which songs and dances were integrated into a dramatic story. It was such a hit with patrons, it ran a then-unprecedented 2,212 performances on Broadway and was made into a movie in 1955, starring Gordon MacRae and Shirley Jones in the lead roles.

Set just outside the town of Claremore, Oklahoma, in 1906, Rodgers & Hammerstein's *Oklahoma!* told the story of a Oklahoma girl who was befuddled by the choices of her suitors. The girl, Laurey Williams, eventually chooses cowboy Curly McLain after a series of escapades and the death of another suitor, villain Jud Fry. Other subplots of relationships are spread throughout the musical, which received a special Pulitzer Prize in 1944 and has won numerous other awards.

While the musical did not win football games, the hit song "Oklahoma!" within the musical became a song associated with Oklahoma football and the Pride of Oklahoma Band. "Oklahoma!" the song was adopted by the Oklahoma legislature as the official state song on May 11, 1953.

Shortly thereafter coach Bud Wilkinson's football Sooners began the longest winning streak in college football history on October 10, 1953, with a 19–14 victory over Texas in Dallas. The Sooners would not lose a football game for more than four years and would win two national championships during the 47-game winning streak. It was truly a magical era for a state that had been characterized as forlorn.

To this day, the song is played at every OU home football game and is generally associated with the football team. It is also played at other athletic contests in the state of Oklahoma by other schools, such as Oklahoma State University.

The mood in the 1950s in the state of Oklahoma was that of resurgence after the Dust Bowl days of the Great Depression in the 1930s and the trying times everywhere during World War II. As much as the John Steinbeck novel *The Grapes of Wrath* depicted the failure of the Oklahoma land in dust and grime and the movement

"Oklahoma!"

Oklahoma, where the wind comes sweepin' down the plain
And the wavin' wheat can sure smell sweet
When the wind comes right behind the rain.
Oklahoma, Ev'ry night my honey lamb and I
Sit alone and talk and watch a hawk
Makin' lazy circles in the sky.
We know we belong to the land
And the land we belong to is grand!
And when we say
Yeeow! Ayipioeeay!
We're only sayin'
You're doin' fine, Oklahoma!
Oklahoma O.K.

—Lyrics to the hit song from the musical Oklahoma!, Rodgers & Hammerstein, 1943

of Oklahoma families to California in the 1930s to find land and work, the celebration of *Oklahoma!* marked hope.

The success of Sooners football, intertwined with the hit musical and the success of the New York Yankees with two other Oklahomans, Mickey Mantle and Allie Reynolds, pushed the state into a new era of prosperity. The fact that Oklahoma now was a state the football team could be proud of seemed to be a prevailing attitude 50 years after statehood had been granted.

38 J.D. Roberts

Give J.D. a call. Oklahoma's second Outland Winner is still going strong and enjoys talking about the old days under Bud Wilkinson.

He still lives in Oklahoma City and makes frequent trips to Texas for business.

It took 56 years, but Oklahoma's second Outland Trophy winner, J.D. Roberts, finally received his trophy on January 15, 2009, during a banquet in Omaha, Nebraska. When Roberts won the trophy in 1953, the Football Writers Association of America presented the Outland winners only plaques.

The FWAA didn't start handing out Outland Trophies until the late 1980s. And gradually during the last decade, the FWAA, in conjunction with the Greater Omaha Sports Committee and Downtown Omaha Rotary Club, has gone back and given former winners their trophies. As the eighth winner of the Outland, Roberts' number came up in 2009.

Roberts, past 80, still waxes poetic about the golden era of Wilkinson, either as a player out of Dallas Jesuit High School, at OU as a starter from 1951 to 1953, or later as an assistant coach under Wilkinson during the 1958 and 1959 seasons.

Roberts was aggressive because of his size, the Sooners compiled a 25–4–2 record during his three seasons. He was quick and disrupted opposing offenses with his knowledge of blocking. Roberts played at 5'10" and around 200 pounds.

"My senior year, they asked me to get down to 200 pounds, which I did," Roberts recalled in 2008. "And I went to Marine camp the summer before my senior season, I lost 15 more pounds. I played my senior season at about 190. They thought I would be quicker. And from the nose guard position I would be able to get off the block quicker."

Roberts can remember every Sooners game during his three seasons, but when you only lose four during your varsity career, the losses are easier to pinpoint than many of the lopsided victories. Two of his first three games as a Sooner were losses in 1951—to Texas A&M and Texas.

"When we played Texas A&M [in College Station], the thing that hurt us was their punter," Roberts said of a 14–7 loss. "He kept us in a hole all night long. No matter where he punted from, we were behind our 20." The next game, a 9–7 loss to Texas in Dallas, OU star running back Billy Vessels got hurt and was lost for the season. "We should have won both games," Roberts said.

The other two losses during his career were both to Notre Dame, one as a junior and one as a senior. He was thrown out at Notre Dame in 1952, a 27–21 loss in South Bend, a sign of how aggressively he tended to play.

"In 1952 it was a couple of minutes before the half, and I got into a confrontation with one of their guards," Roberts said. "He hit me in the back, and I turned and swung at him. And the play was over. I jumped and tried to hit him with a forearm right in the jaw. It was near the Notre Dame sideline. And I remember Notre Dame coach [Frank] Leahy hollering, 'Throw the lad out! Throw the lad out!' I remember the official coming over and saying, 'You're out, son.'

"I had to walk off that field. I had gotten held several times and had gotten hit from behind several times. I finally had had enough of it. I felt very guilty about it. I apologized to my teammates for losing my temper. Coach Wilkinson told me I had to learn to keep my poise."

In 1953 Roberts was hobbled by a preseason thigh injury before the 28–21 loss to the Fighting Irish to begin the season. But after a tie at Pitt, the Sooners won nine straight to begin their 47-game winning streak. The Sooners were the top rushing team in college football in 1953 (306.9 yards a game). In his last college game, Oklahoma pulled a 7–0 upset of national champion Maryland in the January 1, 1954, Orange Bowl.

Upon graduation, Roberts was drafted in the 17th round (195th overall) by the Green Bay Packers, but wound up playing briefly with the Hamilton Tiger Cats in Canada. After also serving in the U.S. Marines, he then went into coaching and was at assistant at Oklahoma, Denver, Navy, Auburn, and Houston before becoming head coach of the New Orleans Saints from 1970 to 1972.

39 OU's Orange Bowl Legacy

Oklahoma's relationship with the Orange Bowl began with the 1938 season when the Sooners made their first bowl trip anywhere and were shut out by Tennessee 17–0 on January 1, 1939. A quarter of a century later, Oklahoma can count 19 trips to the South Florida bowl.

That's more trips to the Orange Bowl than any other team, including fellow Big 12 Conference member Nebraska, which has made 17 trips. The Cornhuskers actually played Oklahoma in the January 1, 1979, game and lost to the Sooners 31–24 after beating OU earlier in the season in Lincoln.

For more than 40 years, from the early 1950s until the mid-1990s, the Big 7/Big 8 Conference had various agreements to send its top teams or its champion to Miami, accounting for the numerous trips of the two juggernaut programs.

Four times, Oklahoma's national title teams have played in the Orange Bowl—1955, 1975, 1985, and 2000—with the later three teams winning the championship there. Oklahoma also defeated the Terrapins 20–6 in the 1956 Orange Bowl after the 1955 season, but the title was not at stake.

In the 1954 Orange Bowl Oklahoma actually defeated national champion Maryland 7–0, but in those days the national title was decided before the bowls. Bud Wilkinson's Oklahoma teams would have played in even more Orange Bowls had the league not had a no-repeat rule in the 1950s.

Three other times (1987, 2004, and 2008), Oklahoma has lost the national title in the Orange Bowl when it dropped games to Miami (Fla.), USC, and Florida. Oklahoma beat Florida State 13–2 in the 2001 Orange Bowl to win its most recent national title under Bob Stoops.

The Sooners have several Orange Bowl Hall of Famers: coaches Bud Wilkinson and Barry Switzer; tight end Keith Jackson; defensive tackle Lee Roy Selmon; running backs Tommy McDonald, Prentice Gautt, Steve Owens, and Billy Sims; and quarterbacks J.C. Watts and Steve Davis.

In the mid- to late 1980s, the Sooners became an Orange Bowl fixture when they won or tied for four straight Big 8 championships, from 1984 to 1987. Overall, from the 1975 season through the 1987 season, the Sooners played in nine out of 13 Orange Bowls. Oklahoma fans began to grumble they were tired of traveling to Miami, and wanted the Big 8 Conference to explore other bowl tie-ins for its champion.

"Barry said there is only one way that you can look at this," said Steve Hatchell, the Orange Bowl's executive director from 1987 to 1993. "He said, 'We have to feel very fortunate we can go to the Orange Bowl. At some point this is going to stop, and people will ask, "When will we get to go back to the Orange Bowl?"' He stopped all that conversation. And sure enough, they didn't come back for a long time."

Oklahoma went from the 1988 season through the 1999 season without an Orange Bowl appearance as Switzer was ousted as coach following the 1988 season. Coach Gary Gibbs never made it there when he was coach from 1989 to 1994. And a coaching carousel and average or poor seasons extended through the 1998 season.

Bob Stoops assumed the Oklahoma coaching reins with the 1999 season. In his second season, 2000, Stoops had OU in the Orange Bowl playing for—and winning—the national title against Florida State.

40 Mascots, Colors, Names, and Trophies

Crimson and Cream

In 1895, the same year the University of Oklahoma started playing football, a committee to choose the school colors was formed. Oklahoma's football team played only one game in 1895, a 34–0 loss to Oklahoma City, but at least the school colors were decided.

The committee, chaired by Miss May Overstreet, decided on crimson and cream and displayed the colors to the Oklahoma student body. The display of the colors was overwhelmingly well-received. The colors began to show up all over the university campus—although the 1895 version of the school was much smaller, four faculty members and 100 students—and the city of Norman.

Eventually, the colors became more of a white and red, but crimson and cream are synonymous with the OU winning tradition.

The Origin of the Name "Sooner"

It's a unique nickname in college or professional sports: Sooner. The word "Sooner" is tied to the development of Oklahoma first as a territory, then as a state in 1907. It was officially adopted as the school's nickname in 1908, coinciding with the fourth year of the Bennie Owen era.

Nearly two decades before statehood, the Oklahoma Territory offered free land to anyone who could make it to the region and stake a claim. The Land Run of 1889 had one rule: all people seeking to stake a claim on the prairie land had to start at one time. A cannon would boom, and everybody would be off.

The settlers who started on time were known as "Boomers," and the ones who started on their wagons or horses too soon were called "Sooners." Hence the arrival of the nickname, which also become associated with progression and the state of Oklahoma as a land of opportunity.

The Golden Hat

The most important one-game, regular-season trophy the Sooners can hoist is the Golden Hat Trophy, which has been awarded to the winner of the Oklahoma-Texas game each year since the 1941 game at the Cotton Bowl.

That year a genuine 10-gallon felt hat was donated by the State Fair of Texas in recognition of the game being played at the Fair Park Stadium during the State Fair each year in early October. The State Fair of Texas had the original hat bronzed, and the trophy became known as the "Bronze Hat." In 1969 the State Fair had the hat replated in gold, and it became the Golden Hat Trophy, which resides at the winning athletics department each season.

Other trophies have popped up over the years, including the Governor's Trophy and the Red River Shootout Trophy (exchanged between the two student bodies). But the Golden Hat Trophy has a special place in the memories of the winning teams and fans. It is normally paraded around the field by the winners, who often wear the Golden Hat.

Mex the Dog: A Popular Mutt

One of the Sooners' early mascots for football and baseball games from 1915 to 1928 was Mex the Dog, a Boston terrier who wore a red sweater with the letter "O" on the side. Mex was originally discovered during the Mexican Revolution along the border near Laredo, Texas, on the Mexican side. A U.S. Army medic, Mott Keys, found the abandoned puppy, and his company took ownership of the dog.

After his military duty concluded, Keys took Mex back to Oklahoma with him and eventually enrolled at the University of Oklahoma. Because of Keys' experience as a medic, he was asked to help with the OU football team and wound up living in the Kappa Sigma fraternity house with Mex. With Mex on the sideline with Keys, fans noticed the dog, who would bark as the crowd roared for touchdowns.

In 1924 Mex received national attention after Oklahoma lost a 28–0 decision to Drake in Des Moines, Iowa. Mex failed to make the train in Arkansas City, Kansas, to complete the trip back to Oklahoma. He was finally found by some Oklahoma graduates at the train station in Arkansas City. They drove him to the Sooners' next game against Oklahoma A&M, a 6–0 Sooners loss during a dreary 2–5–1 season. Four years later, in 1928, the highly popular mascot passed away. Students mourned. Classes were cancelled. And he was buried somewhere near the present OU stadium.

Little Red: Unfashionable Mascot

Protests by Native Americans over the use of Indian mascots occurred 40 years ago in Norman, Oklahoma. In recent years, the NCAA has become involved in doing away with Native American mascots and in some cases nicknames at such places as Illinois, Arkansas State, and Louisiana-Monroe. But OU was well ahead of the curve in Native American relations.

In the early 1950s Little Red appeared at Oklahoma football games as a complement to the Big Red football team. Actually, Caucasians were dressed in red tights, breech cloth, and a war bonnet. Little Red was a sideline cheerleader. Later actual Native

Americans took up the role. But in 1969 Native American students on the Norman campus formed a chapter of the National Indian Youth Council and demanded the removal of Little Red. By the mid-1970s, Little Red was gone.

41 Jammal Brown

OU's 2004 Outland Trophy winner Jammal Brown grew up in Lawton, Oklahoma, but that didn't mean he always had the Oklahoma Sooners on his mind. As a youth, he cheered for the Florida State Seminoles. And he thought about following in the footsteps of another Lawton star lineman, Will Shields, who attended crosstown Lawton High School, later became a Nebraska Cornhuskers star lineman, and won the Outland Trophy in 1992.

One of the reasons Oklahoma was hardly prominent in Brown's mind was the struggles the Sooners were having on the football field in the 1990s under coaches Howard Schnellenberger and John Blake. Finally, coach Bob Stoops arrived in 1999. And Brown decided to give Oklahoma a try because the program was on the upswing.

At the end of his college career, Brown was a two-time All-American in 2003 and 2004 and All–Big 12 three times at right tackle. His senior year, Brown paved the way for running back Adrian Peterson and protected quarterback Jason White, both Heisman Trophy finalists. The Sooners completed a second-consecutive undefeated regular season and won the 2004 Big 12 Conference championship.

Brown led the team in knockdowns and did not allow a sack or a quarterback hurry the entire 2004 season when the Sooners' offensive line surrendered just seven sacks in 13 games. He allowed only one sack in 2003. He led Oklahoma in blocking consistency for two years, and earned the highest grade among the school's blockers in 20 of his final 26 contests. And as a senior, he helped the Sooners average more than 462 yards of offense and led the team with 130 knockdowns.

"I play a physical game," said the 6'6", 313-pound Brown when he won the 2004 Outland Trophy. "It is all a part of it. I want defensive linemen and linebackers to know I am going to be nasty."

Brown played both offense and defense in high school. And when he first arrived at OU, he was on the defensive line. Suffering knee injuries early as a freshman, he sat out in 2000 as Oklahoma won the national title. When he came back the next fall, Oklahoma coaches asked him to move to offense because they had standout defensive linemen in Tommie Harris and Dusty Dvoracek.

Brown thought about transferring to Miami or Tennessee, but accepted the move and stuck it out on the offensive line. And by his sophomore year of 2002 he became a starter at right tackle and was on the road to stardom his junior and senior years.

"Jammal is as deserving of the Outland Trophy as any player we have ever nominated for this award," Oklahoma coach Bob Stoops said. "His performance has been dominating. We all sit in the film room and are amazed at what he does."

Brown was the 13th overall pick in the 2005 NFL Draft by the New Orleans Saints. He played in two Pro Bowls during his career in New Orleans before he was traded in the summer of 2010 to Washington, where he played three seasons. He entered the 2014 season as a free-agent.

42 Keeping the OU-Texas Game in Dallas

For now, the annual game between OU and Texas will not move out of Dallas until after at least 2020 because of agreements among the two schools and the City of Dallas. But there may always be that threat in the future to move the game to campus sites.

Coach Barry Switzer and OU officials really started the talk of taking the Oklahoma-Texas game out of Dallas prior to the 1987 game. Tired of the Dallas media's stories about alleged OU cheating—some of which were later deemed legitimate by the NCAA, which put Oklahoma on probation in 1989—Switzer made news when he said the game should be played on campus sites instead of Cotton Bowl Stadium.

Switzer's threat lingered through different coaching and athletics director regimes in Norman. But no one would pull the trigger. Texas remained politically correct and said nothing. But Texas and Oklahoma would complain about some of the broken pipes, flooding of restrooms, limited entrances, crowded corridors, and lack of enough concession areas in the aging stadium. Plus, the actual seating and scoreboards needed improvements and updating.

"There had been no major construction in 50 to 60 years," said Errol McKoy, former president of the State Fair of Texas.

Later it became more of an economic concern to the two schools, as their stadiums' seating on their campuses began to exceed the Cotton Bowl's 75,000 seats, which are split between the two schools right down the middle. Plus, there were the costs of travel and housing.

Over the years, in order to keep the game at the Cotton Bowl, the City of Dallas had to make improvements to the infrastructure

Did You Know?
Jack Mitchell, OU's quarterback in 1948, was tired of getting tackled carrying the ball during the annual grudge match against Texas. So, before he got tackled, he would pitch it, and the halfback would pick up yardage. This worked in the 20–14 victory over the Longhorns. OU coach Bud Wilkinson got the idea to continue the practice—the option.

of the stadium, increase the capacity, and sweeten the financial pot for the two schools.

In 2007, an agreement included $57 million in renovations to the Cotton Bowl and an expansion of 16,000 seats (8,000 to each team) to 92,200. The agreement also included an approximate $400,000 subsidy paid to each school according to the *Dallas Morning News.*

"The schools said they wanted more seats because of the contributions coming to the universities [for the rights to the tickets]," McKoy said. "The more you donate, the closer to the 50 you get. This game can generate more income than 95 percent of the games in college football."

Oklahoma and Texas players and fans alike now enjoy a stadium that has a new scoreboard and video screen, new aluminum seats, new common areas, wider concourses, more concession stands and restrooms, expanded locker rooms, and a new media room. The additional seats were all in the upper stands and form a completely enclosed bowl. There were also lighting, utility, and sound upgrades.

In 2008 a then record Cotton Bowl Stadium crowd of 92,182 watched No. 5 Texas beat top-ranked Oklahoma 45–35, at the time the highest-scoring game in the then 103-year history of the series. From 2009 through 2013, all the crowds in Dallas have surpassed that total and reached 96,009 on three occasions.

In the spring of 2012, a similar agreement was extended to 2020, with further improvements guaranteed by the City of Dallas to the press box and concourses, plus club seating.

A few years after he resigned as the Sooners' head coach, Switzer admitted that the series belonged in Dallas, which is about equidistant between the two schools. The game has been held at the Fair Park site since 1929 and has become a fixture with the State Fair of Texas each year.

"No football game anywhere comes close to approximating the excitement, the intensity, the pride, the clean play, the fans," said Donnie Duncan, former Oklahoma athletics director and one-time Sooners assistant football coach. "The OU-Texas game exists [in Dallas] because it is supposed to exist. It is something that should not be lost."

"A home-and-home would be like a home-and-home with Nebraska," Switzer said. "You'd get 5,000 seats when we were up there. They would get 5,000 seats when they came down here. There is no influx of monies into the state. Texas is going to stay there in Dallas."

It is also a Texas high school recruiting boon for Oklahoma to play a game in the Dallas–Fort Worth area.

"Spot" Geyer

One of the early University of Oklahoma football stars was 6'2", 172-pound fullback Spot Geyer, from New Haven, Kansas. As a senior, he helped Oklahoma win its first Southwest Intercollegiate Athletic Conference title in 1915 with a 3–0 league record. That team also posted Oklahoma's first double-digit victory season (10–0), the best in school history at that point.

Forest Geyer was known as a "spot" passer, hence his nickname. He was considered the first great passer in Sooners history. One of his teammates said Geyer could throw a "ball 50 yards and hit a nickel with it every time." He could spot a pass behind defenders and throw while running to either sideline.

Geyer would throw the ball as many as 35 times in a game under coach Bennie Owen, who went against the grain in college football in that era by passing the ball. In the Southwest, Owen was known as an early proponent of the forward pass.

Geyer also became known for his passing duels with Texas' Clyde Littlefield, who would later become the head coach of the Longhorns. In 1912 college football rules were relaxed to make the forward pass a more integral part of the game. And two years later in the Oklahoma-Texas game, Geyer and Littlefield tangled.

In the 1914 game Texas won 32–7. Littlefield had the upper hand by completing touchdown passes of 51, 33, and 30 yards. But Geyer suffered an injury to his throwing arm in the game. That would be Oklahoma's only loss in a 9–1–1 season, which included a 96–6 victory over East Central.

The following season in Dallas, Geyer was the dominant figure in the game when he passed 30 times and completed 10 of those for 232 yards in the Sooners' 14–13 victory over Texas. Texas coach Dave Allerdice called the 1915 game the "most thrilling exhibition of passing ever seen in the West."

Texas went ahead 13–7 in the third quarter but missed the extra point. Geyer directed Oklahoma into Texas territory twice, but the Sooners came away with no points. Finally, with about three minutes left in the game, Geyer found Hap Johnson on a 20-yard touchdown pass to tie the score 13–13. Geyer then kicked the extra point for the victory.

Geyer, a geology major, was named All-America at the end of the season by several publications, as unbeaten Oklahoma led the country in scoring. Geyer dabbled in coaching after graduation, but later became the president of an oil company. He died at age 39 in 1932. Forty-one years later, he was inducted into the College Football Hall of Fame.

The Boz

A true Oklahoma fan should certainly watch *Stone Cold* (1991), which is probably the best of several movies in which Brian Bosworth, the former OU football star, has appeared.

Besides being one of the great college linebackers of all time, Bosworth more than anything signified the brashness of the Oklahoma football program in the mid-1980s. In the vernacular of sports, Bosworth could walk the walk after talking the talk. And he liked to talk.

Just ask Texas.

Before the game in 1984, when No. 1 Texas met No. 3 Oklahoma in Dallas, Bosworth, then a star freshman linebacker from Irving, Texas, a Dallas suburb, provided all the bulletin board material the Longhorns would need.

"I don't like Texas," Bosworth was quoted as saying. "I don't like [Texas coach] Fred Akers. I don't like the city of Austin. And I don't like the color orange. It reminds me of puke."

Oklahoma's offensive coordinator Mack Brown, later the Texas head coach, was dismayed that Bosworth would provide Texas with such incentive. Head coach Barry Switzer told Brown, "Both teams will run into each other like two Mack trucks are going to hit each other right in the face. It never matters what they say before the game, so don't worry about it."

That game ended in a 15–15 tie. But 6'2", 248-pound Bosworth won the Butkus Award (best linebacker in the country) as a sophomore and junior. And the Sooners beat Texas 14–7 in 1985 on the way to the national title before they crushed the Longhorns 47–12 in 1986. Boz walked the walk after talking the talk.

A consensus All-American in 1985 and 1986, Bosworth finished his three-year career at Oklahoma with 413 tackles (39 tackles for 191 yards in losses). Oklahoma won three straight Big 8 titles and went to three consecutive Orange Bowls.

While Bosworth's play was superlative, he was always a loose shooter. His Boz-cut radical hairstyles, earrings, and wraparound blue shades reflected his flamboyancy. By the end of his junior year, No. 44's days at Oklahoma were up. Although he was an excellent student and graduated early, he wound up ineligible for the January 1, 1987, Orange Bowl game against Arkansas, a 42–8 OU victory, when he tested positive for steroids. He actually wore a T-shirt on the Orange Bowl sideline that year that said "NCAA: National Communists Against Athletes."

After that episode, he bypassed his senior season at OU, entered the NFL's supplemental draft, and was selected by the Seattle Seahawks. He signed what was then the largest rookie contract in NFL history, worth $11 million over 10 years. But he played only three seasons in the NFL and had to retire because of a shoulder injury—never reaching the heights he did at Oklahoma.

"He was not a good, but a great football player, who led by his actions," said Donnie Duncan, OU's athletics director while Bosworth was a player. "But some of the things that drew attention to him created problems with the policies and procedures with the Big 8 and the NCAA.... That put me in a position believing that shouldn't happen and couldn't happen.

Brian Bosworth discusses the NFL supplemental draft at a news conference in New York after he was selected by the Seattle Seahawks in June 1987.

"The big picture is you are representing a first-class university. And those things don't go together. He was not a dirty player. He was a great team player, a great practice player, a leader. He was just a football player who had WWF [World Wrestling Federation] ideas about the way to draw attention to himself, which in the long run probably enhanced his pocketbook."

To that end, Bosworth had interesting revelations in his September 1988 book, *The Boz: Confessions of an Anti-Hero*. He depicted the scene at OU in the mid 1980s—drug use, guns, and

NCAA violations that later proved true when the Sooners were placed on probation and Switzer was forced to resign in 1989.

Shortly after retiring from the NFL in 1989, Bosworth began appearing in a series of tough-guy movies, the first of which was *Stone Cold*, in which he was an undercover cop who infiltrated a gang of outlaw bikers. Among the other films or productions he has appeared in are *Black Out* (1996), *One Man's Justice* (1996), *Back in Business* (1997), *Three Kings* (1999), and *The Longest Yard* (2005). Bosworth now lives, ironically, in Austin, Texas, and is in private business.

45 Chuck Fairbanks

After the shocking death of coach Jim Mackenzie from a heart attack in April 1967, Chuck Fairbanks, the defensive backfield coach under Mackenzie, was promoted to head coach. Thus began an up-and-down, six-year run for OU football.

On the surface, Fairbanks' 52–15–1 OU coaching record with five bowls, three Big 8 titles, and three national rankings in the top three in the country would look fine. But, remember, this is Norman. And Sooners fans were anxious to return to the heydays of Bud Wilkinson in the 1940s and 1950s.

Fairbanks, the former Michigan State end under Biggie Munn and Duffy Daugherty, at least lent stability to the OU program after it had three head coaches in four seasons prior to Fairbanks taking the top job. From 1963 to 1966, Wilkinson, Gomer Jones (Wilkinson's line coach), and Mackenzie held the coaching reins. During that four-year period, OU was 23–17–1 and failed to win a Big 8 title.

That changed in 1967, when Fairbanks guided the Sooners to a 10–1 record, a Big 8 title, and an Orange Bowl victory over Tennessee. Steve Owens was a sophomore running back on a team that was quarterbacked by Bob Warmack and led defensively by nose guard Granville Liggins.

But the 1968 and 1969 seasons both were inconsistent. OU suffered four losses each season. And the hated Longhorns were rolling with a new offense. In 1968, after a slow start, Texas switched to the wishbone offense. Texas won the last nine games of 1968 and a national championship in 1969, and beat OU both years with it.

Bumper stickers were out in Norman and elsewhere: "Chuck Chuck."

Barry Switzer, then an OU assistant, suggested to Fairbanks that OU switch to the wishbone offense. Fairbanks called his old coach, Biggie Munn, who gave his blessing. Oklahoma unveiled it on October 10, 1970, in a 41–9 loss to Texas at the Cotton Bowl. OU went 7–4–1 that season, which ended with a 24–24 tie against Alabama in the Bluebonnet Bowl. But by the next season with senior quarterback Jack Mildren and junior running backs Greg Pruitt and Joe Wylie, the Sooners rushed for an NCAA record 472.4 yards a game and led the nation in scoring (44.9 points per game).

"I didn't dream it would [be as successful]," said Jim Dickey, an assistant coach at Oklahoma from 1969 to 1972. "It certainly made us good. The first year there were bumper stickers, 'Chuck Chuck.' The next year we were scoring 50 and 60 points in some games. People didn't know what was going on. Darrell Royal had gotten all of those wins. We got it off Darrell, and it was very, very successful."

Fairbanks' final two teams both went 11–1 and finished ranked among the top three teams in the country. The only loss in 1971 was to Nebraska, 35–31, in the Game of the Century. The loss in

1972 was at Colorado, 20–14. After the 1972 season, Fairbanks left to become coach of the New England Patriots, and Switzer ascended to the head-coaching spot and took the Sooners to great heights.

The 1972 season, which resulted in a Big 8 title for the Sooners, was later marred by the Sooners' forfeiture of three Big 8 Conference games, thus giving the title to Nebraska. An Oklahoma assistant coach had falsified the transcripts of quarterback Kerry Jackson. And besides the forfeits, Oklahoma was placed on a two-year NCAA probation and was banned from bowl games in 1973 and 1974 and regular-season television in 1974 and 1975.

46 OU's Dark Side

Every Oklahoma fan must remember that the Sooners have not built one of the powerhouse football programs of all-time without some rocky times along the way (i.e., some of OU's boosters, coaches, and players have been naughty boys over the years). Major NCAA infractions have occurred under all three of the Sooners' top coaches: Bud Wilkinson (1947–1963), Barry Switzer (1973–1988), and Bob Stoops (1999–present).

According to the NCAA's official probation log, Oklahoma ranks tied for third with eight other schools in terms of major infractions cases, with seven. Six of those Oklahoma cases have involved football; the other basketball. No. 1 Arizona State and No. 2 Southern Methodist University are at the top of the list with nine and eight, respectively (all sports). Auburn, Florida State, California, Memphis, Texas A&M, Minnesota, Wisconsin, and Wichita State join the Sooners in the third slot with seven.

January 11, 1956—The NCAA found that the OU football team violated rules regarding improper transportation, extra benefits, and improper recruiting inducements. OU received a one-year probation.

January 11, 1960—The NCAA found that the OU football team violated rules regarding improper financial aid, improper recruiting inducements, outside funding, and lack of institutional control. OU received a one-year probation, a one-year bowl ban, and a one-year television ban.

September 20, 1973—The NCAA found that the OU football team violated rules regarding extra benefits, including improper recruiting inducements; lodging, publicity, and transportation; tryouts; excessive number of official visits; excessive time for official visits; academic fraud; eligibility; and unethical conduct. OU received a two-year probation, a two-year bowl ban, a two-year television ban, and one assistant football coach was not allowed to recruit.

November 11, 1980—The NCAA found that the University of Oklahoma football team violated rules regarding improper financial aid; and improper recruiting contacts, entertainment, and transportation. OU received a public reprimand.

December 19, 1988—The NCAA found that the OU football team violated rules regarding improper transportation; extra benefits; complimentary tickets; improper recruiting contacts, employment, entertainment, inducements, and transportation; unethical conduct; outside funding; lack of institutional control; and certification of compliance. OU received NCAA sanctions as follows: three years probation, one-year television ban, two-year postseason ban; maximum of 18 initial grants for 1989–1990 and 1990–1991 football season; maximum of eight coaches may recruit off campus for 1989–1990; OU limited to maximum of 50 official visits for 1988–1989 and 1989–1990; the University of Oklahoma files annual reports regarding compliance programs; University of Oklahoma must show cause why more penalties should not be imposed if institution does not remove two assistant coaches and recruiting coordinator from recruiting, and disassociate one representative.

July 11, 2007—The NCAA found that OU had violations in the football program involving impermissible extra benefits payment for work not performed and failure to monitor. Oklahoma self-imposed some penalties, including declaring the two athletes involved ineligible and disassociating from the athletics department for five years the manager in the auto dealership involved. OU received public reprimand and censure; two additional years of probation (extended to May 23, 2010); reduced by two the total number of grants it may offer in football for both the 2008–2009 and 2009–2010 academic years; and annual compliance reporting required.

47 OU's First Bowl Team

Oklahoma didn't make its first bowl trip until the 1938 season. And then it took some persuasion by the Orange Bowl's Earnie Seiler, the founder of the bowl and its first business manager and executive director, for the Sooners to pick the Orange Bowl.

Seiler attracted unbeaten Oklahoma to South Florida by making a trip to the Norman campus. And he had to fight off suitors from the Cotton, Sugar, and Rose Bowls, who all had far more lucrative guarantees at the time. Not to be detoured, Seiler had slogans, written with chalk on sidewalks, such as "On to Miami" and "See You at the Orange Bowl," according to the Orange Bowl's official history.

J.D. Roberts on the Cotton Bowl Sideline

Oklahoma won its fifth straight outright Big 7 title in 1952, J.D. Roberts' junior season, but the Sooners did not go to bowl for a second straight season. Roberts said OU was not invited to a bowl in 1951, despite an 8–2 record. The 1952 season was a different matter for an 8–1–1 team, which led the nation in scoring (40.7 points a game).

Prior to 1951, Oklahoma had played in three straight Sugar Bowls following the 1948 to 1950 seasons.

"After the 1952 season, [Oklahoma president] Dr. [George] Cross said no [to bowl games], 'We have been to enough bowl games,'" Roberts recalled. "That was just too much. There was a big oil tycoon down in Ardmore, Oklahoma, who was really mad about it. And he offered to pay all the expenses if he would let us go to a bowl and let the university take all the money from the bowl game. He [the oil tycoon] was on the Board of Regents. And Dr. Cross said, 'No way.'"

With the holidays free, Roberts went home to Dallas. Texas, the Southwest Conference champion which OU had beaten 49–20 earlier at the Cotton Bowl Stadium, was playing Tennessee in the Cotton Bowl. He went to the team hotel to meet friends and ran into Texas assistant coach Bully Gilstrap, who offered him a spot on the sideline. Roberts accepted and watched UT beat the Volunteers 16–0.

In addition, Seiler also lectured the Sooners about Miami and displayed huge posters with girls "reclining on sugary Miami beaches." The Sooners boys took the bait. And the Orange Bowl wound up with a showcase game when unbeaten No. 2 Tennessee elected to play the No. 4 Sooners.

Oklahoma's Tom Stidham was only in his second season as head coach in Norman, but he was part of Seiler's maneuvering since he was a friend of Tennessee coach, General Robert Neyland. Seiler asked Stidham to convince Neyland to play in Miami. And when he did sway the Tennessee coach to do so, the Orange Bowl was overwhelmed by ticket requests and had to turn away 10,000 people.

As it was, a crowd of 32,191 fans jammed into the 22,050-seat Orange Bowl Stadium. There were 5,000 temporary bleacher seats erected in each end zone to accommodate the crowd for a game that truly put the five-year-old Orange Bowl into the big time.

Both Oklahoma and Tennessee were defensive juggernauts during the 1938 season.

Oklahoma, led by its first consensus All-America end Waddy Young, had allowed only 12 points during the entire regular season on the way to the Sooners' second 10-victory season in its history and its first Big 6 Conference football title. The Sooners edged Rice 7–6 in their season opener. Tulsa scored the other touchdown in a 28–6 OU victory. Oklahoma shut out eight opponents, including all five in the Big 6. Tennessee had hurled seven shutouts in its unbeaten season.

Tennessee registered its eighth shutout of the season when it beat OU 17–0. The Volunteers led 10–0 at halftime. Oklahoma managed just 81 yards of offense to Tennessee's 268. But the Sooners were without two injured backfield starters—tailback Howard "Red" McCarty and wingback Bill Jennings.

Tennessee punted 12 times to Oklahoma's 13, but still managed a decent offensive output. Penalties prevailed—242 yards' worth, 157 on Tennessee and 85 on the Sooners. Several players were thrown out of the game because of fighting. Tempers rose in the second half.

Some Oklahoma players were so embarrassed by being shut out, they got off the train on the other side of the tracks when it hit Norman, Oklahoma. And Stidham, who had been the line coach under Biff Jones before taking over the head job, already had shown his displeasure.

After the Orange Bowl loss, Stidham, a native Oklahoman who was one-sixteenth Creek Indian and grew up in Checotah, took off the gray suit he had worn the first 10 games of the season—all victories. He then tossed it out his fifth-floor window.

48 Claude Reeds

Reeds, a 6'2", 170-pound fullback, began the tradition of Oklahoma All-Americans by being the first one in 1913 during his senior season as a Sooner. The Norman native played four seasons, from 1910 to 1913, and was an All-Southwestern pick three of those seasons.

Reeds would have won a sportsmanship trophy if one had been given out during those days. As the first nationally recognized player under coach Bennie Owen, Reeds was known as the "gentleman" of the Southwest.

In his College Football Hall of Fame introduction in 1961, he was remembered as a player this way: "A perfectionist on the gridiron who preferred to play the game hard, but in the most sportsmanship-like manner, Reeds made it all look easy, using uncanny timing and quick reflexes to dart through opposing defenses, like water flowing through a sieve."

But Owen said Reeds was very unselfish and also used him at end, where he was outstanding. "He was the best shoulder blocker, I ever saw," Owen said.

Reeds would confuse opposing defenses by throwing on the run and then also surprising defenses by turning and running upfield for big gains. He was at his best perhaps during the 1911 season when Oklahoma posted an 8–0 record. The Sooners that season outscored the opposition 282–15, including a 104–0 victory over Kingfisher College.

Also an excellent punter, Reeds actually had a punt of 102 yards in 1911 in a 6–3 victory over Texas. At that point the field was 110 yards long, before it was shortened to 100 yards in 1912.

One run by Reeds remains paramount in the memory of historians. It was the final game of his senior season of 1913. He took a fake punt 70 yards for a score in a 14–3 victory over the Buffaloes. Observers said he must have run 200 yards on that fake because he zig-zagged across the field to elude would-be Colorado tacklers.

Reeds was an assistant coach at several small colleges and later became the head coach at Central Oklahoma State, where he won eight Oklahoma Collegiate Conference championships in 10 seasons.

Reeds was inducted into the College Football Hall of Fame in 1961. He passed away at the age of 83 in 1974.

49 OU's 1948 and 1949 Teams

Oklahoma's 47-game winning streak, from 1953 to 1957, gets most of the attention when Sooners football history is discussed. And the 1950 Sooners won the school's first national championship. So that team usually gets its due as well.

But coach Bud Wilkinson's 1948 and 1949 teams (his second and third teams as the Sooners' head coach) were a combined 21–1 and finished No. 5 in the Associated Press rankings in 1948 (10–1) and No. 2 in 1949 (11–0). During this time, Oklahoma put together the eighth-longest winning streak in college football history (31 games). It started with the second game of the 1948 season and extended through the 1950 regular season, ending with a 13–7 Sugar Bowl loss to Kentucky on January 1, 1951.

Oklahoma opened that 1948 season with a 20–17 loss to Santa Clara on the West Coast then won the next nine regular-season games and posted a 14–6 win over North Carolina in the Sugar

Bowl. In the final 1948 AP poll, which was taken before the bowl games, Oklahoma finished behind Michigan, Notre Dame, North Carolina, and California. Wilkinson's 1948 team was stocked with World War II veterans who were older and had grown up long before they were out of college. Those included quarterback, punter, and defensive back Darrell Royal, quarterback and punt returner Jack Mitchell, and end Jim Owens—three All-Americans who would ultimately become head coaches elsewhere.

In 1948 the Sooners ended eight years of frustration by beating Texas 20–14. The last victory over the hated Longhorns had occurred in 1939, two years before the outbreak of World War II. Oklahoma linebacker Myrle Greathouse, another World War II veteran, led a strong OU defensive surge in the 1948 Texas game.

Another talented two-way player in 1948 was senior guard Paul Burris, a three-time All-American, who was OU's line mainstay from Muskogee, Oklahoma. He was the first of four Burris brothers to play at Oklahoma.

Wilkinson's split-T/option was also peaking in 1948, averaging 43.4 points in league games. He had the luxury of three solid quarterbacks on his team with Royal, Mitchell, and Claude Arnold, who actually had started his career at OU in the early 1940s before World War II intervened. George Thomas, a halfback, was the leading rusher on the team with 866 yards and nine touchdowns.

Much of the 1948 team returned the following year, including 1949 All-America tackle Wade Walker, who was one of the top blockers in college football, and 1949 All-America guard Stanley West, who would play seven seasons in the NFL.

In 1949 Oklahoma trailed only an unbeaten Notre Dame team in the polls. The Sooners led the nation in rushing defense (55.6 yards a game). They beat Texas 20–14, the same score as the previous year, when Royal led the Sooners to 20 straight points behind a solid running game.

Thomas, who later played for the Washington Redskins and was a member of OU's winning 440-yard relay team in the 1949 Texas Relays, capped off his four-year career with 15 rushing touchdowns and five receptions. Owens, in his senior season, caught the winning touchdown pass from Royal in the Texas game. And Royal continued to be UT's triple threat at quarterback, defensive back, and punter for one last All-America season.

In 1949 Oklahoma shut out five opponents and gave up only single touchdowns in two other games. The Sooners avenged their 1948 loss to Santa Clara by beating the West Coast team in Norman 28–21. And, after winning the Sugar Bowl for a second straight season, Oklahoma had a 21-game winning streak heading into 1950.

It was truly one of OU's great teams.

50 Landry's Shootouts

Oklahoma's shootout 50–49 victory over West Virginia was of historic proportions during the 2012 season. Landry Jones is one of the best quarterbacks in OU history despite the fact he never won a national title and managed just one conference title team in his four seasons.

The 6'4" 218-pound Jones passed for a school-record 554 yards against the Mountaineers in 2012, breaking his previous record of 505 yards against Kansas State during the 2011 season. He also threw six touchdowns passes, which tied another OU mark he had set as a freshman against Tulsa in 2009.

Jones became, at the time, the third quarterback in FBS history to pass for 3,000 or more yards each of his four seasons,

Landry in OU's Record Books
(Top 10 Sooner passing performances)

1. Jones vs. West Virginia (2012) 554 yards
2. Jones vs. Kansas State (2011) 505 yards
3. Jones vs. Oklahoma State (2012) 500 yards
4t. Jones vs. Oklahoma State (2010) 468 yards
   Sam Bradford vs. Kansas (2008) 468 yards
6. Jones vs. Colorado (2010) 453 yards
7. Jones vs. Missouri (2011) 448 yards
8. Jones vs. Baylor (2011) 447 yards
9t. Josh Heupel vs. Louisville (1999) 429 yards
   Jones vs. Connecticut (2010 season) 429 yards

joining Boise State's Kellen Moore and Hawaii's Timmy Chang on the NCAA's elite list. During the West Virginia game, Landry completed seven passes of 23 yards or more, including one for a 76-yard touchdown. But one of his shortest passes won the game, a five-yarder to Kenny Stills with 24 seconds remaining on a fourth-and-three play that gave the Sooners the pulsating victory.

"It was kind of neat to see Landry audible out to him when he had to there for the touchdown," Oklahoma coach Bob Stoops said. "Kenny ran a great route and fought his way to get the inside position. Those are tough catches when people are hanging all over you."

During his four-year career from 2009 through 2012, Jones had three games with more than 500 yards passing, 12 with more than 400, and 27 with 300 or more yards. He had 123 touchdown passes during this career, 35 more than Heisman Trophy winner Sam Bradford, who played only three seasons and also battled injuries that reduced his number of games.

"He is one of the most unselfish people I know," Oklahoma center Gabe Ikard said of Jones. "He has great character, is always looking out for other people. He came back [his senior season] to lead us to a national championship. But we dropped some games against some really good teams…

"Obviously, Landry was one of the most underappreciated talents we have had around here, just setting all kinds of records. All he got was criticism about us losing games when normally it wasn't even much of his fault."

Jones was selected in the fourth round in the 2013 NFL Draft by the Pittsburgh Steelers. He finished his OU career owning most of the top 10 passing games in Oklahoma football history. All have occurred in the past 15 seasons under Stoops.

51 The Kick

Oklahoma and Ohio State did not play one another until the 1977 season, but at the Horseshoe in Columbus, Ohio, they played a game for the ages on September 24 of that year. It was such a great game—no matter who won—that it is even listed in the book, *Greatest Moments in Ohio State Football History.*

How Oklahoma coach Barry Switzer approached the game very well could have led to the victory—clearly one of the greatest in OU history, considering the setting, the circumstances, and the ending. The game had a tremendous buildup because of its intersectional interest between No. 3 OU and No. 4 Ohio State: Big 8 versus Big Ten. Barry Switzer versus Woody Hayes. A regional television audience on ABC watched the two titans of college football clash.

And it really was a clash of football cultures between the two schools.

"On the Friday afternoon, the Ohio State team is out there doing very highly regimented calisthenics and regular drills," remembers Steve Hatchell, an associate Big 8 commissioner who made the trip. "And the Sooners come out, and they are throwing Frisbees and playing shadow football and pretending you are throwing like it is slow-motion football. These guys are falling all over each over and half goofy. He just did not let pressure get to them."

Oklahoma shot out to a 20–0 lead against the Buckeyes only to watch Ohio State score 28 straight points in the second and third quarters to take a 28–20 lead. The Buckeyes, playing before the third-largest Ohio State crowd in history at that point (88,119), appeared to be headed to victory. Oklahoma then exploded for nine points in the final 1:29 of the game to steal the victory.

OU running back Elvis Peacock scored on a one-yard run to bring OU within 28–26, but he was stopped short on a two-point conversion try. On the ensuing exchange, OU's Mike Babb recovered an onside kick.

"We still have video of this game," Hatchell said. "The Sooners got really beat up in this game. I think Billy Sims got beat up. Dean Blevins [a reserve] was the quarterback late in the game. They have run out of running backs; they are out of people."

Blevins, one of three quarterbacks the Sooners used in the game, directed OU down to the Ohio State 24 with six seconds left. Oklahoma called timeout to send German-born Uwe von Schamann to kick the eventual game-winner from 41 yards. Ohio State then called timeout to try and freeze the kicker, who lived in Fort Worth, Texas.

"And here is Uwe von Schamann in the middle of the field leading the 88,000 people in, 'Block that kick! Block that kick!' moving his arms up and down, and he is the kicker," Hatchell said. "And he lines up and kicks it for the win. The great thing in that game, and we put this in the Big 8 highlight film, here are 11 Ohio State guys lying on the field after the game. Barry's deal was the game is over, let's move on, let's go get a beer."

Standing on the sideline as an assistant coach, Donnie Duncan vividly recalls what he was thinking as von Schamann kicked the ball through the uprights to beat Ohio State.

"There was no one mentally tougher," Duncan said. "I was not surprised when he [led the Ohio State cheer] and when he kicked the ball through. And you know something else—he *certainly* wasn't."

52 Bummer Sooner (USC Belts OU in BCS Title Game)

Auburn coach Tommy Tuberville was in the Orange Bowl press box just in case, reminding writers that his No. 3 Tigers finished 13–0 and shouldn't be left out of a national title consideration. Never mind it was Oklahoma and USC playing on the field.

Then top-ranked USC destroyed previously unbeaten Oklahoma 55–19 in the Bowl Championship Series 1-2 game, removing any doubt as to who was No. 1 among the voters. Not Oklahoma, which suffered one of the most devastating and embarrassing losses in school history and dropped to No. 3 in the final AP poll behind Auburn.

It was the Sooners' second straight loss in a BCS title game. And senior quarterback Jason White's final game as a Sooner was the second of those. It was also the final game for the 2004 Outland Trophy winner, offensive tackle Jammal Brown.

"We just got whipped," Oklahoma coach Bob Stoops said. "You really soul search as a coach how this could happen."

It was the fourth time in Sooners' history an Oklahoma team had entered a bowl game with an unbeaten record and lost. And this was a blowout, unlike the other three losses. The 36-point

Oklahoma Unbeaten Regular-Season Teams (That Have Lost in Bowl Games)

Year	Record	Opponent	Score	Bowl
1938	10–0	Tennessee	17–0	Orange Bowl
1950	10–0	Kentucky	13–7	Sugar Bowl
1987	11–0	Miami (Fla.)	20–14	Orange Bowl
2004	12–0	USC	55–19	Orange Bowl (BCS Title Game)

defeat to USC remains the most lopsided loss of the Stoops era. It was the worst bowl loss in Sooners history, surpassing 31–6 defeats to Arkansas in the 1978 Orange Bowl and to BYU in the 1994 Copper Bowl.

USC quarterback Matt Leinart, the 2004 Heisman Trophy winner, shredded the Oklahoma secondary for an Orange Bowl record five touchdown passes as the Trojans won the national title. The Sooners had five turnovers, including a fumbled punt that set up USC to go ahead for good, 14–7. USC converted the Sooners' turnovers into 31 points. USC tailback Reggie Bush said he felt sorry for the fans who had paid big dollars for tickets and didn't see a competitive game.

"You can't get in these big games and make mistakes like we did," Stoops said. "The turnovers early in a big game like this, you can't have them, and also you can't give up big plays. In the end, that was it. That was the biggest part of it. I'd like to think we can take care of some of that. It wasn't real complicated to do so, and we didn't get it done."

Oklahoma trailed 38–10 at halftime as USC was on its way to gaining 525 yards of total offense against a Sooners defense that had allowed only two field goals in its previous three games. Leinart had 332 yards passing. And USC had 11 plays of at least 12 yards, including Leinart passes of 33, 50, and 54 yards.

Oklahoma's freshman running back Adrian Peterson became the leading freshman ball-carrier in terms of yards gained (1,925) in college football history. But he managed just 82 yards on 25 carries. After the game, Peterson was as stunned as the rest of the team, fans, and state of Oklahoma.

"My mind was blank," Peterson said. "I was in a little daze, my own little world. I was not really thinking of playing football."

53 Jerry Tubbs

Oklahoma began pumping its Texas pipeline for players after World War II. And by the time the mid-1950s rolled around, it was gushing with standouts—but maybe none better than Breckenridge, Texas' Jerry Tubbs.

"Jerry Tubbs made All-America with me and also got drafted by the Chicago [Cardinals of the NFL]," OU teammate Tommy McDonald said. "What a middle linebacker he was. He had speed and very good quickness. And he had [a good] attitude. I think attitude has a lot to do with it. You want to feel like you want be the best on the field you can be. That's the attitude I had—be the best you can be and be better than the best."

The 6'2", 205-pound Tubbs, who later played for the expansion Dallas Cowboys from 1960 to 1966, was part of the celebrated 1956 OU senior class. Tubbs, along with McDonald, quarterback Jimmy Harris, and several others, were 31–0 and won two national titles and three Big 7 championships as sophomores, juniors, and seniors (freshman were not eligible for the varsity).

Entering the 1954 season, coach Bud Wilkinson knew how good Tubbs was because he had seen him as a freshman. The problem was in 1954, college football was one-platoon, and Tubbs was a center on offense. He also had one of the best senior centers in the country in Kurt Burris, who would become a consensus All-America center-linebacker at the end of the season. Tubbs also played linebacker. So how could he keep both in the game at the same time when players had to play offense and defense. Limited substitution rules had been reinstituted in 1953.

"I saw Bud make a great move," said 1953 Outland Trophy winner J.D. Roberts, by then an OU graduate assistant coach. "So whoever you are going to start, you are going to start your senior. Kurt had the experience. And I remember in a staff meeting, Bud saying, 'We have to get those guys on the field at the same time.'

"So he thought the best thing to do, since Kurt was a senior, was to ask Jerry to [move from center on offense and] play fullback that year because that way we could have both of them in at linebacker in the game at the same time," Roberts remembered. "They were probably the two best linebackers in the country, the best pair. He called Jerry in, and Jerry agreed to go to fullback. So when we went on defense, we had Jerry playing the right linebacker and Kurt playing left linebacker."

The Sooners' 1954 defense shut out four opponents and allowed three other teams only seven points or less. The entire season, Texas gave up only 62 points or 6.2 points a game. The most scored against the OU defense was 16 by TCU. And Tubbs was a solid fullback on offense.

In 1955, after Burris had graduated, Tubbs returned to center, but he had established himself as a great defensive player. As an example, in 1955 Tubbs intercepted three passes in a 20–0 victory over Texas. And on offense, he was a star blocker at center and also at linebacker in the Sooners' 20–6 victory over Maryland in the January 1, 1956, Orange Bowl. That win put an exclamation point on OU's 1955 national championship season.

Miami Daily News writer Ralph Warner wrote, "Jerry Tubbs took the decision over Bob Pellegrini, the Maryland All-America, in the battle of the centers. Pellegrini was outstanding, but Tubbs was even more so with a brilliant all-around performance."

In 1956 Tubbs was named an All-America as center-linebacker and was fourth in the Heisman Trophy balloting behind Notre Dame quarterback Paul Hornung, Tennessee halfback Johnny Majors, and OU teammate McDonald. After a 53–0 victory over Oklahoma State, Oklahoma won a second straight national title. The late Tubbs was selected No. 10 overall by the Chicago Cardinals in the 1957 NFL Draft. After his career in the NFL and a 21-year assistant coaching tenure with the Dallas Cowboys, he was inducted into the College Football Hall of Fame in 1996.

54 A Change at Quarterback

Early in the 1953 season, coach Bud Wilkinson made the decision to change starting quarterbacks. The decision process started on the plane ride back to Oklahoma after a 7–7 tie at Pittsburgh. Standing 0–1–1 after two games, the Sooners' offense didn't move the ball against the Panthers with sensational sophomore Buddy Leake at quarterback.

Leake had come from Memphis, Tennessee, and was a flashy athlete. But running Wilkinson's split-T option took precision decision making, not flamboyance. During the tie against the Panthers, senior offensive guard J.D. Roberts, who would win the Outland Trophy that season, had jumped Leake's case a couple of times during the game. Other players could see the two players jawing at each other on the sideline, as could Wilkinson.

"Buddy said, 'Jess don't tell me how to call the game,'" one player in the huddle remembered. "'Buddy you are not using our

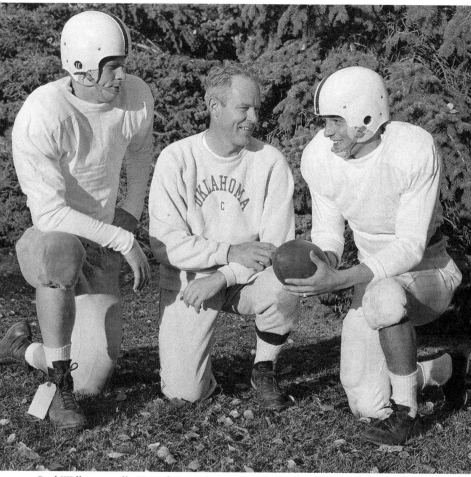

Bud Wilkinson talks Xs and Os with quarterback Gene Calame, right, and center Gene Mears before a workout at the Lafayette M. Hughes Estate in Denver, Colorado, on October 28, 1954.

plays properly, you are calling our 74s and 75s into the field, you don't do that. You call it into the sideline—we don't run into the wide field. We want to run into the sideline. We want to get them in an over-shift.'"

After the game, the ever-wise Wilkinson had sent assistant coach Gomer Jones to the back of the plane to summon a player

Wilkinson's Unique Double Triple

Bud Wilkinson is the only person in college football history who has played on three national title teams and also been the head coach of three national championship squads. Wilkinson was a guard and quarterback for Bernie Bierman's Minnesota Golden Gophers from 1934 to 1936, when they won three straight national titles. At Oklahoma, he coached national title teams in 1950, 1955, and 1956.

to come up and talk to him at the front of the Braniff plane. Wilkinson wanted to ask his opinion about changing quarterbacks for the game the next week against Texas, a make-or-break game for the Sooners. The player told Wilkinson it would be a positive thing for the team if a change was made at quarterback. Wilkinson took the opinion under consideration.

The next week, on Tuesday, as the Sooners were getting ready for Texas, Wilkinson called the OU starting team out and announced that junior Gene Calame, from Sulphur, Oklahoma, would be the starting quarterback and Leake would move to halfback, a position he had played earlier. Calame would win the remaining nine games in 1953 as a starter and was starting quarterback as a senior the next season until he got hurt. Jimmy Harris then took over.

Calame's father was a coach, so he was well-schooled in taking orders. "Buddy had been a heck of a high school athlete in Memphis," one OU player said. "Buddy is one heck of a football player and one heck of a halfback, but at quarterback he was still thinking like a halfback and not like a quarterback.... He wasn't really running our offense like the man wanted."

Wilkinson's hunch paid off. The 1953 Sooners, with Leake back at halfback and Calame running the show, led the country in rushing with 306.9 yards a game. After a 19–14 victory over Texas, Oklahoma scored 30 or more points five times and then upset national champion Maryland 7–0 in the Orange Bowl.

55 Darrell Royal

He grew up in the Dust Bowl days of the Great Depression in Oklahoma. His mother, Katy, died of cancer when he was an infant. His family moved to California to pick fruit at one point, but Darrell returned to live with his grandmother and became a football, basketball, and baseball star at Hollis High School. His life was right out of *The Grapes of Wrath*.

He grew up listening to OU football games on the radio in the 1930s while playing football in his front yard. "Boomer Sooner!" would blare all over the neighborhood. Later, when he was older, Royal once saw Indian Jack Jacobs, a top quarterback-punter-defensive back for the Sooners from 1939 to 1941 at Owen Field, and that helped make his decision to eventually play for the Sooners.

But right out of high school in 1943, Royal enlisted in the Air Force and attained the rank of staff sergeant during World War II. Like many other World War II veterans, he returned to Oklahoma ready to play college football and was a 22-year-old freshman in the fall of 1946.

Everything clicked at Oklahoma. Royal was an important part of the beginning of the Sooners' football dynasty. They won conference championships in each of his four seasons (possible because freshmen were eligible to play after World War II).

Royal united with Bud Wilkinson in 1946 when Wilkinson was the Sooners' backfield coach for one season under head coach Jim Tatum before Tatum left to become the head coach at Maryland. Wilkinson then became the Sooners' head coach in 1947. Royal played halfback his first two seasons and was a quarterback his final two seasons. He was named an All-American in 1949, his senior year, when Oklahoma went 11–0 and beat LSU 35–0 in the Sugar Bowl.

Royal was excellent at running the split-T option play, but split time his first three seasons with Jack Mitchell and then Claude Arnold. In 1949, as a senior full-time starter in 11 games (all OU victories), Royal passed for 509 yards and rushed for another 195 yards. And Royal, like Jacobs several years before him, was a tremendous punter and defensive back.

In 1948 against Oklahoma State, Royal had an 81-yard punt, which was an OU record at the time and still ranks as tied for the third-longest punt in Sooners history. The same year against Kansas State, he had a 96-yard punt return for a touchdown that is still the longest in school history. His 18 career interceptions have never been equaled at OU. And his three interceptions in a game has only been tied—but not surpassed—by several OU defenders.

Royal was drafted by the New York Bulldogs in the 1950 draft, but instead went into coaching, where he became a Hall of Famer. He eventually landed the head-coaching job at the University of Texas, Oklahoma's biggest rival. And he was one of the central figures in that game for two decades. As an Oklahoma player, he had a 2–2 record against Texas. As a Texas head coach from 1957 to 1976, he was 12–7–1 and won eight straight games over his alma mater from 1958 to 1965.

With a 167–47–5 overall record with the Longhorns, Royal won three national titles at Texas, the same number won by Barry Switzer and Bud Wilkinson at Oklahoma.

Royal's background from the Dust Bowl days in Oklahoma gave him a folksy nature to complement his coaching pedigree. He became legendary for such sayings as, "Dance with the one that brung ya," "Football doesn't build character, it eliminates weak ones," or, "You've got to be in a position for luck to happen. Luck doesn't go around looking for stumblebum."

Royal passed away in 2012 at the age of 88.

56 Tom Osborne

Nebraska's legendary coach Bob Devaney beat Oklahoma the last two times he coached against them, including the 1971 Game of the Century. But his successor, Tom Osborne, who was on the sideline for that 1971 game in Norman, didn't have success early in his career in the late-season showdown games with OU.

Promoted from assistant to head coach in 1973 after Devaney retired, Osborne lost his first five games against Oklahoma from 1973 to 1977 by scores of 27–0, 28–14, 35–10, 20–17, and 38–7. During that span, the Sooners either won or tied for every Big 8 title and won national championships in 1974 and 1975.

"When we did start beating Coach Osborne, he knew we had gotten into their heads," former OU quarterback Dean Blevins said. "He never talked negatively about a team. He always held Nebraska in the greatest light. But he knew in the fourth quarter [we could win]. He would say, 'Do you think they really can beat you? Hell, no.' And they didn't."

Osborne's Cornhuskers finally beat No. 1–ranked Oklahoma 17–14 in 1978. But even then, Osborne could not enjoy it much. The next week Missouri upset Nebraska 35–31. With Oklahoma and Nebraska tied for the Big 8 title, the Orange Bowl rematched the teams on January 1 in Miami, where Oklahoma prevailed this time, 31–24. Oklahoma won the next two regular-season games 17–14 in 1979 and 21–17 in 1980. "This may be the best one yet," Switzer quipped about the 1980 thriller.

Finally, Osborne won three straight over OU from 1981 to 1983. But OU's Switzer won four of his last five against Nebraska. Overall, he had a 12–5 record versus Osborne, usually in

Play Two Straight at Nebraska? Okay with Barry

In the early 1980s the old Big 8 Conference hierarchy had a request by several schools that their schedules be readjusted so league teams wouldn't play both Oklahoma and Nebraska on their home campuses during the same season. The two Big Reds were the biggest draws in the league. So it was beneficial for schools such as an Iowa State or Kansas to have them coming to Ames and Lawrence, respectively, in different seasons.

"So your ticket sales would be awesome one year and not so good the next," said Steve Hatchell, who was a Big 8 associate commissioner in those days. "If you went out 10 to 12 years, eight to nine years, there was a point Oklahoma had to play at Nebraska two straight years. I remember Wade Walker [Oklahoma athletics director] said, 'We are not going to sit still for that. That's a big paycheck for us [Nebraska home game].' But it would only take place one time.

"I remember Barry coming into the room and saying, 'You are telling me I have to go to Nebraska two years in a row?' Everybody had their head down and their eyes down. It was sort of the deal. And Barry was so smart. He asked, 'Well, will this help the conference?' Well, Barry it will. Barry said, 'I will tell you what, you got to tell Tom he can't play his starters until halftime. Well, we will do that,' he said. 'But at some point you guys owe us something, you owe the Sooners something.'"

And Oklahoma won both games in Lincoln, 20–17 in 1986 and 17–7 in 1987, and two more Big 8 titles.

late-season, high-stakes encounters that determined the conference championship.

"There was all that 'Sooner Magic' stuff," said Adrian Fiala, former Nebraska player and Cornhuskers radio game analyst. "I frankly thought it was a bunch of b.s. Some people bought into that. Sometimes it looked like our guys were kind of out there waiting for it to happen versus playing though it and getting it done. I think for a few years, the thought was, 'Hey, it's inevitable it is going to happen. It probably is going to happen.'"

Oklahoma's Switzer simply may have related better to star players. Nebraska's Osborne appeared to be bedrock: staid, bland,

and consistent. Switzer was quicksand: flamboyant, controversial, and unpredictable. Osborne was the grandson of a Nebraska Presbyterian minister. Switzer was the son of an Arkansas bootlegger. Hence, the contrasts in the way the two programs were run.

Under Osborne, Nebraska's program was structured and closed off to the media to the point it reminded people almost of a fortress. Nebraska's players carried themselves with a certain rigidity, almost military-like. Oklahoma was the Lazy Q Ranch, always open. Players were allowed to display their individuality on and off the field. Interviews and quotes flowed out of Norman like lava. Nebraska's players were usually under lock and key.

"I remember Barry Switzer's famous line, his pregame speech, 'Dear God, don't let the best team win,'" Fiala said.

"I think Oklahoma was extremely talented. And I think Nebraska was starting to come into its own," said Frank Solich, who joined the Cornhuskers staff in 1979. "But Oklahoma had so much speed and so much talent. In those games, I always thought Tom did a great job of coaching and putting our football team in position to have a chance in those games. But when you are up against that much talent, sometimes it just doesn't work."

After Switzer was forced out at Oklahoma following the 1988 season, Osborne went 8–1 against the Sooners against three different coaches between 1989 and 1997, through the end of his coaching career.

57 Paul Young

Center-defensive back Paul Young wore three different numbers (15, 22, and 45) for Oklahoma during the early 1930s. The

Sooners had nondescript football records. And Young, a Norman, Oklahoma, native, would merely be a line in the OU Football Lettermen's section, except that he went on to become one of the most successful high school football coaches in state history.

As a result, Young also delivered some of the state's best players to Bud Wilkinson's powerhouse OU program during the late 1940s and 1950s, including three All-Americans, linemen Bo Bolinger and Kurt Burris and end Max Boydston, who, along with Burris' brother, Bob, were known as the "B Boys" from Muskogee.

After coaching the OU freshman team in 1935, Young became an assistant coach at Ardmore, Oklahoma, in 1936. There, in 10 years as the head coach, he built Ardmore into a state power and then moved on to Muskogee Central High School from 1947 to 1961. Over a 25-year period, Young posted a 174–62–11 high school record and was president of the Oklahoma Coaches Association four times.

Young's best teams were 1948 and 1950 state titlists at Muskogee Central High. The Muskogee team members had been dubbed the "Roughers" after winning a state title in 1925 with rough play. The 1950 Muskogee team finished 13–0 and featured seniors Boydston and Kurt Burris, along with Bob Burris and Bolinger, both underclassmen.

The Burris family of Muskogee became legendary because Young plucked three of the six football-playing brothers out of the same household. And it might have been four sons, but Young didn't arrive in Muskogee early enough. Paul "Buddy" Burris was already at Oklahoma by the time Young arrived in Muskogee. Paul Burris, a guard, was OU's first three-time All-American (1946–1948). The four-brother dynasty of players is unique in OU history for the same era.

Bob Burris, a fullback, lettered from 1953 to 1955. But the other great Muskogee catch was Kurt Burris, the center-linebacker for the Sooners, who was a consensus All-American for the Sooners in 1954 and was second that season in the Heisman Trophy balloting behind Wisconsin fullback Alan Ameche. Coach Young wasn't finished with the Burris pipeline, either. Recruited later, Lynn Burris, a guard, lettered on Oklahoma's 1956 national title team.

Other Muskogee Central High players Young sent to Oklahoma were quarterback-defensive back Eddie Crowder (1950–1952), end Joe Rector (1956–1958), and lineman Jere Durham (1957–1958). Crowder was an All-American in 1952, when he accounted for 930 yards of offense running and throwing, and led the Sooners to an 8–1–1 record and a No. 4 national ranking in both major polls.

For Young's effort as a high school coach, he was inducted into the Oklahoma Sports Hall of Fame in 2001, 31 years after he passed away at age 59.

58 2008 BCS Controversy

Oklahoma prevailed off the field, even if it didn't on it against Texas.

Once-beaten Texas couldn't politic its way to the national title game in 2008—even though it had a win over Oklahoma on its résumé. And the Sooners went to the Big 12 title game and then the Bowl Championship Series national title game against Florida. The Longhorns had to settle for a bid to the Tostitos Fiesta Bowl and no shot at a national title.

The BCS computers were not kind to Texas, which lost to Texas Tech late in the season. That loss on the road to the Red Raiders factored more than the Longhorns' victory over Oklahoma on a neutral field in Dallas.

"Going into the last couple of weeks, we knew that a good team was going to be left out of the Big 12 championship," said then Texas coach Mack Brown. "Unfortunately, in this situation, it was us."

When Oklahoma played Oklahoma State in Stillwater on November 29, Texas fans had a plane fly over Boone Pickens Stadium with the score 45–35 as a reminder that the Longhorns beat Oklahoma by that score in their annual Red River Rivalry game on October 11.

The Sooners were unaffected by the fly-over and pulverized Oklahoma State 61–41 to forge a three-way tie for the Big 12 South Division title with Texas Tech and Texas. The final tiebreaker to determine which team would play North Division title winner Missouri in the Big 12 title game in Kansas City would be decided by the BCS standings the next day.

And the Sooners, with impressive victories over the Cowboys and a smashing 65–21 win over Texas Tech (the team which beat Texas 39–33), leap-frogged the Longhorns into the No. 2 spot in the next-to-last BCS standings used to break the three-way Big 12 South Division tie.

Oklahoma was No. 2 at .9351 and Texas was No. 3 at .9223. The human polls were split on the two teams, but the computers gave the Sooners the edge. That meant the Sooners would get to play Missouri in the Big 12 title game and possibly get a shot to go to the BCS Championship Game.

"Everybody has their opinions," Oklahoma coach Bob Stoops said after the Sooners belted Missouri 62–21 in the Big 12 title game. "Some people's are different than others. That's a pretty convincing win in a championship game when you have to have it against a ranked team. I think that's the fifth ranked team that we've been able to beat this year."

The Big 12 Conference had never encountered such a high-stakes tie for one of its division winners. And it had to go to its fifth tie-breaker to determine the division representative in the title game among the three teams. The catch is that the Southeastern Conference at that time used the BCS standings to drop the lowest-ranking team in a three-way tie, and then determined the division winner by the head-to-head meeting. If that had been the rule in the Big 12, Texas very well might have won the national title.

"Since this situation has never happened before in the Big 12, I think the conference should follow the lead of all of the other BCS leagues with championship games in how they settle three-way ties," Brown added. "I think their systems are fairer and give more credit to how the two highest-ranked teams performed against each other on the field."

The Big 12 Conference reviewed its tiebreaking procedure in the spring of 2009, but the league did not change it. And by the 2011 season, with only 10 teams in the league after the defections of Nebraska to the Big Ten and Colorado to the Pac 12, the title game had been eliminated.

59 Wilkinson vs. Royal in 1958

In 1957 Oklahoma coach Bud Wilkinson came face-to-face with his former Sooners quarterback Darrell Royal (1946–1949) on the floor of the Cotton Bowl on the *opposite side* of the field in the OU-Texas game. It was Royal's first season as head coach at Texas. And top-ranked OU—in the midst of a 47-game winning streak—beat the Longhorns 21–7 for a sixth straight time.

But the 1958 game would be a completely different matter. OU would prevail 15–14 in a titillating game, actually decided by a two-point conversion that had just been introduced into the college game that season. It was a move Wilkinson had pushed for as a member of the NCAA Football Rules Committee, which had met the previous January, according to an account in *Anatomy of a Game* by David Nelson.

The loss to Texas would begin an eight-game Oklahoma losing streak in the series as Royal's Longhorns became a national power and OU fell upon hard times. It truly was a changing of the guard in terms of power in the Southwest, although Texas was a member of the Southwest Conference and OU was in the Big 8.

Oklahoma coach Bud Wilkinson (right) shakes the hand of his former player Darrell Royal as they leave the field in Dallas on October 10, 1959.

Royal, who oddly enough did not approve of the two-point conversion rule because he believed it was unfair to coaches, successfully utilized that option after UT's first touchdown for an 8–0 lead. He knew there would probably be little scoring, so he reasoned why not use it early instead of maybe having to make that decision late in the game.

Oklahoma stormed back to take a 14–8 lead. But late in the game Texas scored on a jump pass from quarterback Bobby Lackey to Bobby Bryant to forge a tie. Lackey also kicked the extra point for what turned out to be the winning margin.

The loss turned the tide. Oklahoma was snakebit in the series and lost to UT 19–12 the following year. Then, in the last four Royal-Wilkinson games, the Sooners never scored more than seven points in any game, losing 24–0 in 1960, 28–7 in 1961, 9–6 in 1962, and 28–7 in 1963. Wilkinson left college coaching for politics in 1963, with a 1–6 record against Royal.

The chances of Oklahoma losing a game to Texas on a controversial rule change that Wilkinson pushed for and actually made a motion for in the meeting was just a side note to what happened that season.

But it could have cost Oklahoma the national championship in what was Wilkinson's last great season in Norman. The Sooners did not lose another game in 1958, finishing 10–1 and beating Syracuse in the Orange Bowl. The Sooners finished fifth in the final polls.

By the 1959 season, even Oklahoma's superiority in conference play became an issue. Wilkinson's Sooners won or tied for a conference championship for a 14th-straight year, but lost their first conference game (25–21 at Nebraska) in the Wilkinson era, which dated to 1947. In 1960 Oklahoma fell to 3–6–1 and never again seriously contended for the national title under Wilkinson, winning only one more league title in 1962.

60 The Bomb Game

It is believed to be a first in college football.

Near the end of the first half of the Kansas State–Oklahoma game on October 1, 2005, a bomb went off near the stadium in an apparent suicide by a University of Oklahoma student. Although play continued and players and many fans at Owen Field didn't realize a bomb had been detonated, the west side of Gaylord Family–Oklahoma Memorial Stadium shook slightly.

And word soon spread throughout the stadium that a bomb had been set off less than hundred yards outside the stadium in a traffic circle area where several busses were parked.

Oklahoma and other Big 12 schools already had plans in place in the case of such an occurrence. Representatives from the FBI; Bureau of Alcohol, Tobacco, Firearms, and Explosives; the Big 12; and the Norman Police Department sprang into action. A command center was actually set up in the novelty shop inside the stadium.

Fans were not allowed to leave the stadium at halftime, as was custom. As authorities tried to sort out what had happened and analyze the scene, the game went on as scheduled. Oklahoma won 43–21 before a crowd of 84,501. But afterward, fans had to exit out of limited gates to the outside. People were asked to exit out the south and east portals, causing great congestion. Traffic also was snarled for several hours after the game as the main road west of the stadium was closed.

The bomb went off near a street oval where a Kansas State bus was parked. The bus was such a mess, it had to be taken to a car wash to be cleaned before it could return to Manhattan, Kansas.

An investigation followed into events and the student himself, Joel "Joe" Henry Hinrichs III, a mechanical engineering student from Colorado Springs, Colorado. Hinrichs had constructed a homemade bomb, which he had in his bag, and had written a suicide note that was left back at his campus apartment.

In July 2006 the FBI issued a report that there was no evidence that Hinrichs, who reportedly suffered from depression, was a terrorist or was working with anyone else to detonate the bomb. But the FBI never determined one way or another if Hinrichs was trying to enter the stadium and commit a mass murder. Many observers believed he was trying to do just that.

Oklahoma tightened security for future home games. Before the next home game on October 22 against Baylor, Oklahoma football season-ticket holders received a letter from OU President David Boren. The letter detailed new stadium security procedures, including restrictions on bags and purses, hand searches, and more security cameras.

61 Headington Hall

Bud Wilkinson Hall was the main athletic dorm on the corner of Jenkins and Lindsey within easy sight of the Gaylord Family–Oklahoma Memorial Stadium. Near the end of the Barry Switzer era the athletic housing facility became infamous for, among other things, the site of a rape by two OU football players.

Now, Bud Wilkinson Hall has been replaced by the $75 million Headington Hall, which was funded by the Oklahoma athletic department and named after a former Sooner tennis player who contributed to the funding of the project. The 230,000-square-foot, five-story Headington Hall is the home to 380 Oklahoma students, 180 of them athletes.

Oklahoma coach Bob Stoops calls it a "game changer" for Oklahoma football, which obviously will benefit his recruiting efforts.

The building consists of two- and four-bedroom apartments, plus a central dining era, computer labs, study rooms, and a theater. While the previous Bud Wilkinson Hall (also referred to at times as Bud Wilkinson House) did not blend into the campus architecture (Cherokee Gothic), Headington Hall does.

"We wanted to create a living and learning experience," said Oklahoma athletic director Joe Castiglione. "We wanted our students and student-athletes to have the greatest possible start to their career from a living perspective. We really tried to be creative and innovative for the residents themselves."

Two of Oklahoma's biggest stars have contributed to the project: quarterback Sam Bradford, the 2008 Heisman Trophy winner, and Adrian Peterson, in 2012 the NFL's Most Valuable Player.

Peterson made a $1 million donation to the Oklahoma athletic department, $500,000 of which was designated to Headington Hall. The $1 million donation is the largest ever made by a former Oklahoma athlete. Peterson's name will be attached to an academic and study lounge.

Peterson said he had always hoped to "donate back to the University of Oklahoma and make it an even better place; do whatever I could to help the university that did so much for me…It was a no-brainer to do it, and I am thankful that I'm in position to give back to OU and to show my appreciation."

Bradford also made a $500,000 contribution to Headington Hall. His name is attached to the Training Table, "a state-of-the-art dining area."

"My experience at Oklahoma made it possible for me to realize my dreams," Bradford said. "The coaches, the academic environment, and every aspect of being a student-athlete at OU made me a better person. I am honored to give back to a program that did so much for me."

Tim Headington is a well-known philanthropist who owns his own diversified company, Dallas-based Headington Resources, which is involved in real estate, hotel development, natural gas, oil, film production, entertainment, and private equity. He was inducted into the Oklahoma (State) Hall of Fame in 2013.

62 2002 Rose Bowl Team

Oklahoma made its 36th bowl appearance in Pasadena on January 1, 2003. The 2002 Sooners were not the Rose Bowl's first choice. In fact, the Rose Bowl officials were upset the FedEx Orange Bowl had maneuvered, through the Bowl Championship Series selection procedures, a Rose Bowl–type matchup of the Big Ten's Iowa and the Pac-10's USC in Florida, some 2,500 miles way.

Despite its storied past and high-octane offense, Oklahoma wasn't exactly viewed as a great catch to play Pac-10 champion Washington State.

The Rose Bowl had hosted its first BCS title game the previous year; Miami (Fla.) had beaten Nebraska for the national title. Thousands of Big Red Nebraska fans had brought their campers and RVs and lined the lots. Oklahoma was just looked at as a second straight Big Red interloper in what had been the Pac-10 and Big Ten's private party before the advent of the BCS in the late 1990s. Those conferences had played in every Rose Bowl since the 1947 game before the Miami-Nebraska matchup.

Adding a tinge of controversy to the game was the fact that Washington State coach Mike Price already had resigned to take the Alabama head coaching job, but he would remain to coach the Cougars in the Rose Bowl. That undoubtedly helped in slowing ticket sales in the state of Washington and resulted in the smallest bowl-game crowd (86,848) at the 105,000-seat Rose Bowl since 68,000 watched USC beat Washington 29–0 on January 1, 1944. Conversely, at the time this was the third-largest crowd to ever see the Sooners play a game.

Oklahoma jumped to a 27–0 lead behind senior quarterback Nate Hybl, who had had an up-and-down career as a Sooner, but was named the player of the game. He passed for 240 yards and had two touchdowns with no interceptions. Oklahoma running back Quentin Griffin, also playing in his final game, had his 10th-straight 100-yard rushing game. Washington State didn't score until the fourth quarter, when the Cougars put two meaningless touchdowns on the board.

Dating to the first half of a 1999 Independence Bowl loss to Ole Miss, Oklahoma had not allowed a touchdown in 13 straight quarters against bowl opponents, including the 13–2 victory over Florida State in the national title game (Orange Bowl) and a 10–3 victory over Arkansas in the Cotton Bowl.

"Defense played another one of those games," Oklahoma coach Bob Stoops said. "We're disappointed we didn't shut them out." The Cougars averaged 437 yards of offense going into the game, but managed only 243 against Oklahoma. They rushed for only four yards.

Although Sooners fans did their part in buying 20,000 tickets to the game, Oklahoma's appearance in the Rose Bowl was looked at somewhat of a disappointment back in Oklahoma. Big 12 champion Oklahoma got knocked out of any possibility of making the BCS title game at the Fiesta Bowl with November losses to Texas A&M and Oklahoma State.

It was the second straight season Oklahoma played in a new bowl. Despite the fact that Oklahoma meets Texas annually in the Cotton Bowl in early October, the Sooners' first bowl-game appearance in Dallas was on January 1, 2002, when they beat Arkansas 10–3.

63 1963 Oklahoma-Texas Game

It was the first time in Oklahoma football history that the Sooners were involved in a game between the No. 1– and No. 2–ranked teams in the country. And it is the only time in the history of the long-running series between the two rivals that the teams have been ranked 1-2.

Oklahoma entered the game as the No. 1–ranked team after dispatching Clemson 31–14 and then–No. 1–ranked USC 17–12 two weeks previously in Los Angeles. Second-ranked Texas was 3–0 and thirsting for atonement after losing to LSU 13–0 on the very same Cotton Bowl field the previous January 1.

Oklahoma was mouthy leading up to the game.

After the USC game, which was televised nationally by CBS, Oklahoma offensive tackle Ralph Neely said in front of the cameras, "Texas, you're next."

Controversial senior OU halfback Joe Don Looney played the final game of his career against Texas, in part because he had punched a graduate assistant coach earlier in the year. He may have been the most talented player never to reach his full potential. The Fort Worth native, who made All-America and led the nation in punting in 1962, predicted the week of the game that UT's offense could not keep with Oklahoma's. That didn't happen.

Looney, who was kicked off the team for good by OU coach Bud Wilkinson before the following week's game against Kansas,

Oklahoma in 1-2 Games (AP Poll)

October 12, 1963
No. 2 Texas 28, No. 1 Oklahoma 7 (Dallas)

November 25, 1971
No. 1 Nebraska 35, No. 2 Oklahoma 31 (Norman)

September 26, 1981
No. 1 USC 28, No. 2 Oklahoma 24 (Los Angeles)

September 27, 1986
No.2 Miami (Fla.) 28, No. 1 Oklahoma 16 (Miami)

November 21, 1987
No. 2 Oklahoma 17, No. 1 Nebraska 7 (Lincoln)

January 1, 1988
No. 2 Miami (Fla.) 20, No. 1 Oklahoma 14 (Orange Bowl, Miami)

January 4, 2005
No. 1 USC 55, No. 2 Oklahoma 19 (Orange Bowl, Miami)

January 8, 2009
No. 1 Florida 24, No. 2 Oklahoma 14 (BCS Title Game, Miami)

rushed for just four yards on six carries. And OU's other running threat, Lance Rentzel, had only 18 yards. This was the game where UT defensive lineman Scott Appleton probably won the Outland Trophy that season because he made 18 tackles. He was honored as the Associated Press Lineman of the Week.

Looneys' comments rang rather hollow in light of the fact that Texas quarterback Duke Carlisle completed just one pass all game, but he was still pictured on the front cover of *Sports Illustrated* the next week.

The Oklahoma-Texas game was part of an unusual big-time double-header weekend at the Cotton Bowl. Before the OU-UT game, fourth-ranked Navy and Roger Staubach lost to SMU 32–28 on Friday night.

The 1963 OU-UT game was the first of eight 1-2 games (in the Associated Press poll) OU has been involved with during its history. The Sooners have won just one of those games, a 17–7 victory over No. 1 Nebraska in 1987 that wrapped up the Big 8 Conference title and sent the Sooners to the Orange Bowl for another 1-2 game with the Miami Hurricanes.

64 Othello's Table of Truth

It's a must stop for any true Sooners fan. Just a chance to see the Barry Switzer's "Table of Truth" is worth the trip.

In the Campus Corner area of Norman, at 434 Buchanan Avenue, Othello's Italian Restaurant is still going strong for dinner each night. Made famous in the days Barry Switzer was OU's head coach.

On game weeks during the regular season, home or away, current OU head coach Bob Stoops usually can be seen at Othello's on Tuesday nights having dinner with his staff. It's a ritual. There's a standing reservation. Sooners football players also often eat at the restaurant.

Othello's has all the old Italian favorites at reasonable prices: lasagna, veal parmesan, veal marsala, spaghetti and meatballs, fettuccine alfredo, etc. Live entertainment and hand-tossed pizzas are signature staples. The food is good and the wine flows, particularly on Friday nights before home football games and Saturday nights after morning or afternoon home football games.

The centerpiece attraction in the restaurant is the "Table of Truth," located in booth in the middle of the restaurant. It has been there for three decades ever since Switzer befriended Othello's former owner Patsy Benso, and he reserved a standing table for Switzer. The wooden-framed table with a tiled top would always be open for him and still is.

Legend has it if you tell a lie while sitting at the table, it will move. A plaque hangs on the wall beside the table, with a couple of inscriptions: "La Tavola della Verita" ("Table of Truth") and "Old Coaches Never Die, They Just Forget How to Score."

Patrons who happen on Othello's can't sit at the Table of Truth, but they can look at a piece of Sooners tradition. The table is reserved for the owners and the owners' friends and some of the regulars.

There is a second location, a much younger franchise spinoff of Othello's at One South Broadway in downtown Edmond, Oklahoma, an Oklahoma City suburb. It also has a Table of Truth that is patterned after the original. Switzer wanted one there as well when he first arrived at the restaurant.

"When we had the grand opening, Coach Switzer came in," said Bob Weiss, the owner of the Othello's in Edmond. "He was looking around and said, 'Bob, where is the Table of Truth?' So we put one in. We always have people asking what is the Table of Truth because we mention it on the menu."

Some of the best dishes at the Edmond location, according to those there, are any pasta smothered in the alfredo sauce and a penne pasta with sliced Italian sausage; green, red, and yellow peppers; and onion in a special marinara sauce.

65 Adrian Peterson

Barry Switzer was in the urinal relieving himself at the Cotton Bowl during the 2004 Oklahoma-Texas game. It was Adrian Peterson's freshman year. Well down the trough line, a Texas fan spotted the King and asked him, "What the hell did you guys pay to get Peterson?"

Switzer, in his usual quick wit, jokingly answered, "Whatever it was, it was worth it, wasn't it?"

Peterson, a 6'1", 217-pound running back from the east Texas town of Palestine, about 100 miles southeast of Dallas, was one of the most highly coveted high school players in the country. And despite an injury-riddled career (2004–2006) in Norman that kept him from becoming the Sooners' career rusher, he still gained 4,041 yards rushing in 31 games. Only Billy Sims and Joe Washington gained more rushing yards as Sooners.

In that 2004 Texas game, which the Sooners won 12–0, Peterson rushed 32 times for 225 yards on the way to 1,925 yards as a freshman. He carried the ball more times (314) than any freshmen in major-college history and for more yards. He had more consecutive 100-yard rushing games (nine) and more total 100-yard rushing games (11) than any freshman in major-college history as well.

"He's an East Texas guy—corn-fed," said Texas linebacker Derrick Johnson. "I mean he's the type of guy raised in a barn... the type of guy who picks up haystacks. He looks like he does that. He's the type of running back that defenses have to try to stop. He can run over people and he will outrun you, too. You've got to wrap him up."

Peterson, who finished second in the 2004 Heisman Trophy balloting to USC quarterback Matt Leinart, was in position to have another huge year in 2005, but he suffered a high ankle sprain in Oklahoma's victory over Kansas State in the fourth game of the season. Despite missing two games and having reduced playing time in two others in 2005, he still managed to rush for 1,104 yards and 14 touchdowns.

Upon his arrival in Norman, Texas native Adrian Peterson was a practically supernatural force at running back for the Sooners.

Included in that total was an incredible second-half performance in a 42–14 Oklahoma triumph over Oklahoma State, in which he carried the ball for 210 yards in the final 30 minutes of the game. It was the best one-half rushing total in Sooners history. Peterson finished with 237 yards and two touchdowns against the Cowboys. His 84-yard jaunt against Oklahoma State was one for his highlight reel.

"I played basketball, I ran track, I did every sport," Peterson said of his high school days and his desire to do well. "No matter what I did, I wanted to be the best. I wanted to be the first—if it was running sprints, lifting weights. That whole attitude just carried on. That's all it is. It's just having an attitude."

In 2006 Peterson, who entered the season just 1,085 career rushing yards behind Sims, had more bad luck. In the sixth game against Iowa State, he scored on a 53-yard run, but when he dove into the end zone, he suffered a broken collarbone. Peterson had another 1,000-yard rushing season, but didn't return until the Tostitos Fiesta Bowl, when he gained 77 yards and fell 73 yards short of Sims' career rushing record and 26 yards behind Washington.

Peterson elected to bypass his senior year at Oklahoma and entered the 2007 NFL Draft. He was selected seventh overall by the Minnesota Vikings. He has gone on to have a star-studded career in Minneapolis.

"He is such a competitive player, and I appreciate so much what he brought to our program," Oklahoma coach Bob Stoops said at the time Peterson was selected by the Vikings. "He has great pride in the way he plays, and he's extremely tough. Those qualities rub off on the people around him. He has the kind of competitive spirit that elevates those around him. It means an awful lot to him that the entire team does well, and I think that is probably his most underappreciated quality."

66 Oklahoma Sports Hall of Fame

The Oklahoma Sports Hall of Fame in Oklahoma City has more Sooner football coaches and players (29) in the two-story, 40,000-square-foot facility than any other team. The five-year-old Hall of Fame is located in Oklahoma City's tourism corridor just north of the State Capitol Building.

"OU fans ought to enjoy exploring the museum because of the rich history and heritage of University of Oklahoma sports displayed here," said Lynne Draper, former executive director of the Jim Thorpe Association, the group that operates the museum and also the fund-raising group for its creation.

"There are great halls of fame to celebrate sports in other states, but no state has the unique sports heritage that Oklahoma does," Draper said. "So this Hall of Fame has been long overdue. It is a source of pride and inspiration for all Oklahomans."

The Oklahoma Sports Hall of Fame and Jim Thorpe Museum, which had a price tag of $8 million, features the Bud Wilkinson Events Center, which is an area that seats several hundred people for weddings, banquets, and graduations. Jay Wilkinson, son of the late great Sooners coach, has donated several items from his father's days as OU football coach to the museum.

Each Sooner in the museum has an an electronic video on his college career and, where applicable, his professional career. The museum also has an archive area with scrapbooks donated by Hall of Famers in various sports.

For example, visitors can view end Waddy Young's All-America Certificate and his Army Air Corps ID Badge in World War II and Sooners running back Clendon Thomas' Pittsburgh Steelers helmet. There are personal artifacts for all the Sooners.

Oklahoma Football in the Hall

Player	Position	Year Inducted
J.C. Watts	Quarterback	2014
Jimmy Harris	Quarterback	2013
Dewey Selmon	Defensive Lineman	2012
Lucious Selmon	Defensive Lineman	2011
Rick Bryan	Defensive Lineman	2010
+Tony Casillas	Defensive Lineman	2008
Tom Catlin	Center	2009
Eddie Crowder	Quarterback/DB	2003
Prentice Gautt	Running Back	2000
Jack Jacobs	Back/Punter	2002
+Keith Jackson	Tight End	2006
Harold Keith	Sports Information Director	1987
+Tommy McDonald	Running Back	1991
Jack Mildren	Quarterback	1998
+Bennie Owen	Head Coach	2001
+Steve Owens	Running Back	1991
+Greg Pruitt	Running Back	1997
+J.D. Roberts	Lineman	1997
*Port Robertson	Wrestling, Support Staff	1995
+Darrell Royal	Quarterback/DB/Punter	1992
+Lee Roy Selmon	Defensive Lineman	1992
+Billy Sims	Running Back	1994
+Barry Switzer	Head Coach	1990
+Clendon Thomas	Running Back/DB	1995
+Jerry Tubbs	Center/Linebacker	1999
+Billy Vessels	Running Back	1989
+Joe Washington	Running Back	1993
+Jim Weatherall	Lineman	2001
Paul Young	DB/Center/H.S. Coach	2001
+Waddy Young	End	2007
+Bud Wilkinson	Head Coach	1986

*Went in for wrestling, but also assisted in football
+Also in College Football Hall of Fame

The museum is open Tuesday through Saturday from 10:00 AM to 5:00 PM. There is also a gift shop and an orientation theater at the museum.

After the 2014 inductions, OU football boasts 26 players, three head coaches, and two football support personnel in the hall.

67 Officiating Controversies

Bring up two particular games from the Bob Stoops era, and Stoops feels like stomping on his visor. Both were on the road. Both involved officiating controversies. And the Sooners lost both during the space of six games spanning the 2005 and 2006 seasons.

The first was a 23–21 loss at Texas Tech on November 19, 2005. The second was about 10 months later, on September 16, 2006—a 34–33 loss at Oregon which might have cost the eventual Big 12 champion Sooners a shot at the national title.

The Oregon game involved two plays, which incredibly were reviewed by Pac-10 officials with instant replay. Later, the Pac-10 Conference office admitted that replay officials and on-field officials erred in one of the instances that determined the outcome of the game. The Pac-10 apologized to Oklahoma after the loss and suspended the officiating crew and replay officials for a game.

Oregon had drawn within 33–27 late in the game and tried an onside kick. Replays later showed an Oregon player interfered with Oklahoma's attempt to recover before the ball traveled the mandatory 10 yards. Thus, Oregon should never have had the ball in a position for the winning drive.

"Errors clearly were made and not corrected, and for that we apologize to the University of Oklahoma, coach Bob Stoops, and his players," said Pac-10 commissioner Tom Hansen. "They played an outstanding college football game, as did Oregon, and it is regrettable that the outcome of the contest was affected by the officiating."

Also, during another play after the Ducks' ruled recovery of the fumble, an OU player was flagged for pass-interference on a tipped pass—a call which would have been negated by rule by the tip. Replays were inconclusive.

Bob Stoops and the Sooners have experienced their share of controversial calls from officials during Stoops' tenure.

"The instant replay was brought up to eliminate issues like this. And here, there are a number of issues that are clearly—looking at video—wrong," Stoops said after reviewing the tapes.

In the Texas Tech loss, three of 12 plays on Texas Tech's game-winning 65-yard drive were reviewed with instant replay—and two critical decisions went against OU.

One appeared to be a poor ball placement on a crucial pass-completion play during the final drive, which was rubber-stamped by the Big 12 replay booth. Another was a five-yard pass from Texas Tech quarterback Cody Hodges to receiver Joel Filani that was ruled a touchdown on the field but overturned as a bobbled incomplete pass by the Big 12 replay booth three plays before the winning touchdown.

But the killer as far as Oklahoma was concerned was the final play of the game. A two-yard touchdown run by Taurean Henderson that won the game for the Red Raiders as time ran out was highly controversial. Video replays reviewing whether Henderson was down and then extended the ball across the goal line were inconclusive, according to the Big 12 replay booth. "I started out to score the touchdown, got hit, was laying on top of someone, and just stretched out," Henderson said.

Oklahoma athletics director Joe Castiglione said the Henderson "touchdown" was strikingly reminiscent of the Famous "Fifth Down" touchdown in 1990 in which Missouri lost 33–31 to Colorado when the Buffaloes received five downs to score a touchdown. Castiglione was a senior associate athletics director at Missouri in charge of game management at the time. Whether Colorado quarterback Charles Johnson ever got in the end zone on fifth down was also in question, as photographs suggest he stuck the ball over his head in the end zone after he already was down on the ground.

68 Riverboat Gambler Bob

In 1999, in his first season as head coach, Oklahoma coach Bob Stoops showed he was a big-time gambler. In a 51–6 throttling of Texas A&M in College Station, his frequent gambles and trick plays totally befuddled the Aggies, who suffered their worst loss since a 46–0 drubbing by Baylor in 1901.

It was just the beginning of Stoops' head coaching career. But he has kept up this gambling nature throughout the first decade of coaching in Norman.

1999—Oklahoma 51, Texas A&M 6. Stoops' first Oklahoma team hadn't finished business in losses at Notre Dame (34–30) and against Texas (38–28) in the previous two games. But the Sooners used a hook-and-lateral and successfully faked a punt and field goal in beating the Aggies in College Station in one of Stoops' big early victories over a ranked team. A 41-yard run on a fake punt set up the first of Tim Duncan's three field goals.

2002—Oklahoma 31, Missouri 24. In a game against Missouri in Columbia, Stoops had no confidence in his kicking game because of wet and long grass. Trailing 24–23 in the fourth quarter, Oklahoma lined up to attempt a 31-yard field goal. Instead, holder Matt McCoy threw a 14-yard touchdown pass to tight end Chris Chester with 6:33 remaining. The Sooners also converted a two-point conversion after the touchdown, which was the knockout punch. Oklahoma won 31–24.

2002—Oklahoma 35, Texas 24. A week later, in Dallas against Texas, Stoops took another gamble, albeit much smaller. Trailing 14–3 right before halftime, Oklahoma was down to possibly just one play with 10 seconds remaining and on the Texas 3.

The safe play would have been to either kick a field goal to make it 14–6 or call a running play and then a quick time out if it didn't work. Instead Nate Hybl threw to Trent Smith for a touchdown with three seconds left in the half. A two-point conversion pass was good, and OU was within three, 14–11. The momentum was OU's. And the Sooners totally dominated the second half.

2003—Oklahoma 20, Alabama 13. At Alabama early in the next season, Stoops saw that momentum shifting again. In the third quarter Alabama had closed within 13–10, and the home crowd of 83,818 was into the game. Oklahoma appeared to be stopped at its 31-yard line on fourth-and-11 and facing a punt. But punter Blake Ferguson passed in the flat to Michael Thompson for a first down, 22 yards to the Alabama 47. The knockout punch was on the next play when Jason White hit Brandon Jones down the sideline on a 47-yard touchdown for a 20–10 lead. Oklahoma wound up winning 20–13.

2008—Texas 45, Oklahoma 35. Against Texas in Dallas again, Stoops rolled the dice. Oklahoma had a fourth-and-six at its own 48 late in the third quarter. Texas had drawn within one, 28–27. Stoops felt the momentum favoring Texas, so he had punter Mike Knall run out of the punt formation. Knall came up one yard short on the fake punt. Texas took over at its 47 and in five plays had the go-ahead field goal and its first lead of the game. Texas went on to win.

2009—Florida 24, Oklahoma 14 (after the 2008 season in the BCS national title game at the Orange Bowl). In the final 10 seconds of the first half, Oklahoma had a chance to take the lead with a field goal when the Sooners' coaching staff elected to go for the touchdown at the Florida 6-yard line. With the scored tied at 7–7, OU quarterback Sam Bradford threw a pass that was batted up into the air and intercepted by Florida short of the goal line. OU came up with zero points. It was the second time in the first half OU had driven inside the 10 (the other was at the 1) and come away empty. OU seemed deflated. Florida took control in the second half.

2013—Oklahoma 33, Oklahoma State 24. It was certainly a momentum play during this Bedlam Series game in Stillwater. In what appeared to be a certain field-goal attempt, Stoops faked the three-pointer when he had holder Grant Bothun keep the ball, swing to the left, and then pass to kicker Michael Hunnicutt for a touchdown. The subsequent extra point tied the score at 17–17 in the third quarter. OU would score twice in the closing minutes to pull out the victory that sent the Sooners to the Sugar Bowl.

69 Jim Owens

Although Jim Owens may have ultimately been selected to the College Football Hall of Fame because he took the University of Washington to three Rose Bowls, his presence as an end on Bud Wilkinson's OU post–World War II juggernaut teams can't be overlooked.

Owens was a lanky 6'4", 205-pounder from Classen High School in Oklahoma City, and an Oklahoma All-State player in 1944. He served in the U.S. Naval Air Corps during World War II and returned to Norman as one of those hardened freshmen playing for coach Jim Tatum in 1946. After Tatum left for Maryland, Owens starred for Wilkinson the next three seasons.

"He undoubtedly was one of the best football players I have ever coached, both offensively and defensively," Wilkinson said in the late 1940s. "He is one of the best tight ends to play college football."

Owens showed what he could do as a freshman in 1946 in the biggest game of the season and in only his third college game when he caught five passes (one for a touchdown) in a 20–13 loss to Texas. During the 1946 season, Owens caught 19 passes, including four for touchdowns, as the Sooners posted an 8–3 record and a 34–13 victory over North Carolina State in the Gator Bowl.

Owens was also one of the best blockers and defenders in college football. In a 27–7 victory over Missouri's Gator Bowl–bound team in 1949, Owens had key blocks on three Sooners touchdowns.

During Owens' junior and senior seasons of 1948 and 1949, the Sooners won 21 of 22 games. They were 10–1 in 1948, losing only to Santa Clara in the season opener, and 11–0 in 1949 when they beat Louisiana State 35–0 in the Sugar Bowl. Owens was a cocaptain and an All-American in 1949 when OU outscored the opposition 399–88. And he caught the winning touchdown pass from quarterback Darrell Royal in the closest game of the 1949 season, a 20–14 victory over Texas.

After graduation, Owens played one season for the Baltimore Colts but already was gravitating toward coaching. He was an assistant for Bear Bryant from 1951 to 1953 at Kentucky and was part of the grueling Junction, Texas, preseason camp in 1954 with Bryant in his first season at Texas A&M. After three seasons in College Station, Owens replaced his Oklahoma teammate Darrell Royal as head coach of the University of Washington Huskies. Royal spent only one season in Washington before taking the Texas job.

In 18 seasons, from 1957 to 1974, at Washington, Owens' teams compiled a 99–82–6 record, won three league titles, and appeared in three Rose Bowls. Owens claimed the Huskies' first Rose Bowl victory in 1960 over Wisconsin 44–8 and followed that up a year later with a 17–7 victory over Minnesota in Pasadena.

Although Owens' coaching tenure was tinged with racial controversy in his dealings with some African American players, five years after he retired, he was inducted into the inaugural class of Washington's sports hall of fame. Owens went into the College Football Hall of Fame in 1982, and in 2003 a statue of him was unveiled in front of Husky Stadium.

70 Sooner Schooner

The Oklahoma Sooner Schooner's most infamous trip on the field occurred in the 1985 Orange Bowl. The Schooner, reminiscent of the Conestoga wagons used in the Oklahoma Territory during the late 1800s, got stuck in front of the Washington Huskies' bench and was flagged for a 15-yard unsportsmanlike penalty.

First used at an Oklahoma game in 1964 at Owen Field and adopted as the school's official mascot in 1980, the Sooner Schooner, with matching white ponies Boomer and Sooner, is administered by the RUF/NEKS, an all-male spirit organization. The Sooner Schooner is driven onto the field at home and bowl games in an arc to the 50-yard line after every score. Principally, there's a driver and the RUF/NEKS' queen sitting in the front and a flag-waving RUF/NEK in the back of the small wagon.

As the Sooners' high-scoring machine has plundered numerous foes during the last 45 years, the Sooner Schooner has made countless trips onto the field without being penalized. But the grass on the Orange Bowl field was in poor condition because of rain during the week, and the wheels got stuck. Washington players lunged at the wagon, and the officials threw a flag when it didn't get off the field quickly enough.

The Sooners had rallied from a 14–0 deficit to tie the score at 14–14. They were prepared to attempt a chip-shot field goal by

Tim Lashar from 22 yards to take a 17–14 lead. The initial kick by Lashar was good, but the Sooners were penalized five yards for illegal procedure. The RUF/NEKS saw the officials' hands go up, signaling the field goal was good. So the Sooner Schooner routinely dashed onto the field.

"Oh, it definitely starts conversations," said Greg Graham, a 1984–1985 RUF/NEK, told the *Seattle Post-Intelligencer* in a 2005 story. "It's been good for 30 or 40 free drinks over the years."

With the 15-yard penalty charged to the Schooner (20 yards total in penalties), Lashar all of a sudden had a tougher-to-make 42-yard field goal, which was blocked. Ultimately, Lashar kicked a 35-yarder for a 17–14 lead in the fourth quarter, but Washington rallied with two fourth-quarter scores to win the game.

"But that wasn't the difference," Oklahoma coach Barry Switzer said after the game of the penalized Sooner Schooner. "It would have been closer. But they were the better team that night."

Another Sooner Schooner–RUF/NEKS incident occurred before the 2004 Nebraska-Oklahoma game in Norman—in pregame warmups. Nebraska's Darren DeLone, a 6'6", 315-pound lineman collided with a RUF/NEK.

The RUF/NEK wound up falling into a brick wall. He injured his head, back, and spine and lost one tooth. Prosecutors alleged that DeLone deliberately ran into 19-year-old Adam Merritt following a verbal altercation between Nebraska players and RUF/NEKS. DeLone was charged with aggravated assault (having acted intentionally), but later was acquitted. Bill Callahan, Nebraska's head coach at the time, called Oklahoma fans "hillbillies" after the game, which the Sooners won 30–3.

71 RUF/NEKS

In 1915 at an Oklahoma basketball game, an elderly female fan was upset by a group of football players who were cheering and being rowdy. She yelled at them, "Sit down and be quiet, you roughnecks!" Thus, a tradition was born. And the RUF/NEKS have since developed numerous traditions over the years in and around Oklahoma football games.

Organized in 1917, the RUF/NEKS were originally a group of Oklahoma independent students. Recently the group came under OU control as an official university spirit organization after allegations of hazing and alcohol abuse surfaced in 2007. They are most visible at Oklahoma football games, home and away.

In 1921 the RUF/NEKS started carrying red-and-white paddles to OU football games. Although the original intent was to encourage OU fans to cheer for the Sooners and also intimidate opposing teams and their fans, more recently the paddles have become a symbol of the RUFF/NEKS' tradition and pride in themselves and the University of Oklahoma.

Starting in 1939, the RUF/NEKS would stand guard over the Oklahoma campus the week before the Oklahoma A&M game. And in 1952 when the OU football team came on the field at the beginning of a game, the RUF/NEKS would hold the paddles in an arch under which the team would run onto the field.

Other traditions also have developed over the years with the RUF/NEKS. "Fadada" is an act where the RUF/NEKS run onto the field with the Oklahoma flags and all slide into the goal post and say a chant. It began early in Sooners football history and was seen as a way of scaring the snakes out of the end zone. Before the

Oklahoma's Biggest Fan

Cecil Samara was undoubtedly Oklahoma's biggest fan. When he passed away in 1994 in his seventies, gone was a fixture of Oklahoma football games for more than 40 years. He had an "O" and a "U" on caps on his front teeth, besides dressing all in red and driving the Red Rocket, a 1923 Model-T Ford, to home football games, often to the Oklahoma-Texas game in Dallas and bowl games.

When he died, he was buried wearing an OU tie, an OU belt buckle, a red jewel OU pin, and a red felt hat at his side. They played "Boomer Sooner" at the funeral and made sure it wasn't on game day, at his request. His casket was draped with U.S., Oklahoma, and OU flags.

Oklahoma-Texas game each year in Dallas, the RUF/NEKS paint "Beat the Hell Out of Texas" on a sidewalk or street.

Another chore is being the keeper of the "Big Red Rocket," a red-and-white 1923 Model-T Ford that has been to every Oklahoma home football game since 1950. Once owned by the late Cecil Samara, who passed away in 1994, the car is now owned by Sissy Tubb, Cecil's daughter. Each year a new keeper of the car is chosen from the RUF/NEKS.

Since the mid-1960s, they have been in charge of the Sooner Schooner and the ponies, Boomer and Sooner, who are driven onto the field after Oklahoma touchdowns. The RUF/NEKS also shoot off modified 12-gauge shotguns in pregame activities. Each year the RUF/NEKS name a new keeper of the guns.

72 Jack Jacobs

Oklahoma's best passer in the early years was Jack Jacobs, who played at Oklahoma from 1939 to 1941 and later was a prolific passer in the NFL and the predecessor of the Canadian Football League. He became known as the legendary "Indian Jack." He played all the running back positions and defensive back, and punted superbly at Oklahoma.

The 6'2", 186-pound Jacobs was a marvelous and fluid athlete. He was a full-blooded Creek Indian, attended Muskogee Central High School, and was an All-State fullback in 1938. Once at Oklahoma, he was a star player, but he probably made more of a name for himself in professional football (as a passer and defensive back) because of greater exposure. OU was only 18–8–1 during his three seasons and never went to a bowl.

Inducted into the Oklahoma Sports Hall of Fame in 2002, Jacobs had a passing motion described as unique: "a quick swoop of the arm above the head, with powerful wrist-action like a baseball catcher's peg to first base when the runner has strayed off the bag."

Remarkably, Jacobs, the Sooners' leading passer during the 1940 and 1941 seasons, averaged 47.84 yards a punt in 1940. Sixty-eight years later, that is still a Sooners record. In 1940 he averaged 52.0 yards a punt in a 14–0 victory over Kansas State and 52.3 yards a punt in a 13–0 loss to Nebraska. His 42.1 yards a punt career average still ranks third at Oklahoma.

Former UT coach Darrell Royal, a native of Hollis, Oklahoma, recalled to University of Texas historian Bill Little how he went to an early Oklahoma football game and was mesmerized by Jack Jacobs, who was also an excellent punter. Royal went to Oklahoma in 1946 and was much the same type of player, as a quarterback, defensive back, and punter.

"I just remember watching 'Indian Jack' Jacobs kick," Royal told Little. "The way he held the ball, the measured steps, the swing of his leg.... I was glued to him."

Jacobs was selected in the second round of the 1942 draft by the then–Cleveland Rams (later of Los Angeles and St. Louis). But because of World War II he went into the Army and played only

10 games for that franchise, from 1942 to 1945. In 1946 he played for the Washington Redskins, and then he played three seasons for the Green Bay Packers. He led the NFL in punting in 1947 with a 43.5-yard average.

His passing opened up the Western Interprovincial Football Union, the forerunner of the Canadian Football League, from 1950 to 1954, when he played for the Winnipeg Blue Bombers and took them to two Grey Cup finals. In 1951 he became (many believe) the first professional quarterback to throw for 3,000 yards in a season (3,248). He also threw 33 touchdowns that season. In all he passed for 104 touchdowns during his career in Canada.

With Jacobs playing quarterback, Winnipeg became a Canadian power, and demand for seats in the city increased to the point a new stadium was needed. Winnipeg Stadium, built in 1953, was known as the "House That Jack Built."

Jacobs was enshrined in the Canadian Football Hall of Fame in 1963, and 14 years later he was inducted into the American Indian Hall of Fame. He was inducted into the Oklahoma Sports Hall of Fame in 2002. He passed away in 1974 at the age of 54.

73 Barry Switzer Center

Certainly anyone wanting to get a great feel for the Oklahoma football program should visit the Barry Switzer Center, located in the south end of Gaylord Family–Oklahoma Memorial Stadium in Norman.

Visitors will find the three-floor Legends Lobby particularly interesting. (It's open to the public from 9:00 AM to 5:00 PM on Thursdays and Fridays of every week, 10:00 AM to 3:00 PM on

Sundays after home football games, and until 6:00 PM on Fridays before home football games.)

The first floor boasts a bust of Barry Switzer and a wall-sized mural depicting the history of Oklahoma football featuring most of the great players and coaches, Memorial Stadium, the Orange Bowl, Cotton Bowl (the Oklahoma-Texas game site), the Pride of Oklahoma Band, fans, cheerleaders, the Sooner Schooner, the National Championship Scoreboard (at Memorial Stadium), and many trophies and rings. The mural is nearly 10 feet high and 32 feet, 9 inches wide and was painted by nationally renowned artist Ted Watts of Oswego, Kansas.

The museum has several historic artifacts, including a fundraising brochure used for the original stadium construction, the ball used to score the first touchdown against Nebraska on Owen Field in 1922, a fan's megaphone from the 1930s, one of Bud Wilkinson's fedoras, a pair of Joe Washington's silver shoes, championship rings presented to Sooners players and coaches, one of Switzer's windbreakers, and a visor worn by Bob Stoops.

The second floor commemorates the team's accomplishments, coaches, and bowl trips. The story of Oklahoma football is told, interspersed with Oklahoma state history. The Oklahoma Land Run, the origins of football starting on campus, and the Sooners' nicknames are featured. National titles are celebrated in kiosks, complete with trophies and other memorabilia. The top coaches—Bennie Owen, Bud Wilkinson, Barry Switzer, and Bob Stoops—are featured on televised panels. There are five more kiosks for the major bowls the Sooners have played in over the years. And dangling from the second-floor ceiling are replicas of bowl program covers.

The third floor is devoted to individual player accomplishments. This is where the five Heisman Trophies are displayed. Oklahoma players have won virtually all the major national individual awards and, in many cases, they have done so multiple times.

Among those trophies on display on the third floor are the Outland Trophy, the Lombardi Trophy, the Butkus Trophy, the Jim Thorpe Trophy, the Bronko Nagurski Trophy, and several others. Another display honors those Sooners who have been inducted into the Pro Football Hall of Fame and those who are first-team Academic All-Americans. On north and south walls of the third floor, all of the Sooners All-Conference players, All-Americans, and OU players with professional careers are recognized. Touch screens are available for visitors to see highlights of the players and learn even more about them.

In the Anderson All-American Plaza outside the Switzer Center, a large wall honors every Oklahoma All-American to wear a Sooners uniform in any sport, and letter-winners from every Oklahoma sport also are listed.

74 Bud's Strategies

Bud Wilkinson's great success at Oklahoma was in large part due to the fact that he organized practices to the minute and had a superior knowledge of the team's personnel. OU's Outland Trophy winner, J.D. Roberts, a lineman from 1951 to 1953, was a graduate assistant shortly after his college career ended and then a full-time assistant for Wilkinson in 1958 and 1959. To this day, Roberts still has his notebook of Wilkinson's practices.

"This was our schedule during two-a-days," Roberts said, reading from his little brown book, a half century old. "We had to be at the locker room at 6:00 AM. We practiced from 6:30 to 8:00 AM. Then we had a 9:30 AM meeting, and that meeting was on personnel and to correct mistakes that we saw. We would go

Wilkinson's Wisdom

Kenny Rawlinson was a longtime trainer at the University of Oklahoma who tended to the football team when Bud Wilkinson was coach. He also was a trainer for the men's basketball team under Dave Bliss. John Underwood, an assistant coach for Bliss, remembers one thing Rawlinson once said about his days under the methodical Wilkinson.

The basketball Sooners were on the road against Oral Roberts in Bliss' second season (1976–1977) in Norman. The Sooners had lost three of four games, and Bliss, a former assistant under Bob Knight at Indiana, had the whip out. He practiced the team an hour and a half on the day of the game. A tired Oklahoma team lost to ORU 68–50.

When Rawlinson was asked what Wilkinson would have done, he responded, "He would have had them rested." Underwood remembers Bliss didn't repeat that mistake again.

to breakfast real quick before the 9:30 meeting. Then we had a players' meeting at 11:00. Then we had a 1:00 staff meeting to get our practice schedule together. Then we had group meetings at 2:30 and we practiced from 4:00 to 6:00. Then right after the practice we had a meeting to get the practice schedule for the next day at 7:30. We would get out of there about 8:30 PM.

"The first meeting we had, he started talking about loyalty among the staff, the players," Roberts said. "The players can sense when the coaching staff lacks loyalty. So he expected total loyalty. Once a decision was made in that meeting room, we all agreed, whether it was your decision or not, we all were on the same page. He wanted us to coach the kids like we would want one of our own kids coached. This was a tough schedule during the whole football season. When you did have time, he expected you to be a family man."

Although Wilkinson tolerated two-platoon football (the way the game is played today) in the early 1950s, he still chose his players to play both ways. College football went back to one-platoon football in 1953 for a period of 12 years.

"In 1950, '51, '52 we were playing two-platoon football like it is today," Roberts said. "In 1953 it was one-platoon, and everybody had to play both ways. Bud didn't like two-platoon football. So everybody on our team had an offensive and defensive position. Now, in the early 1950s we did have some guys who only played only offense. And we had guys who only played defense.

"The way he picked the team was by defense," Roberts said. "Who did he think was his best middle guard or nose guard, as they called it today? That guy was going to be the right guard on offense. Who was your best left tackle on defense? He was going to be your left guard. Who is your best left end? He is going to be the left tackle. And your fullback was going to be your right linebacker, and your center was going to be your left linebacker. Even during two-platoon football, everyone played offense and defense. We didn't scrimmage like the No. 1 offensive team against the No. 1 defensive team. We couldn't because there were two or three of us who played both ways. Everybody had two positions."

75 Pride of Oklahoma Band

A must for any Sooners fan is to watch the Pride of Oklahoma Band either in concert or at a Sooners football game; they perform before and after the games and, of course, at halftime. The band has a long history of being associated with University of Oklahoma football.

In the early years, around the turn of the 20th century, citizens of Norman and University of Oklahoma students formed a pep band at home football games. But the band would break apart after the football season due to an inability to afford sheet music.

"Boomer Sooner"

The University of Oklahoma's college fight song was written in 1905, two years before Oklahoma became a state, but a decade after the beginning of the football program in 1895. The adoption of the fight song coincided with the first season of Coach Bennie Owen, who remained as Oklahoma's head coach through the 1926 season.

Arthur Alden, a University of Oklahoma history and physiology student, wrote the lyrics, but the tune was actually taken from Yale University's song, "Boola Boola." A year after Alden's adaptation, the words of University of North Carolina's "I'm a Tar Heel Born" were added to the lyrics, substituting Sooner and Oklahoma.

Boomer Sooner, Boomer Sooner
Boomer Sooner, Boomer Sooner
Boomer Sooner, Boomer Sooner
Boomer Sooner, OK U!
Oklahoma, Oklahoma
Oklahoma, Oklahoma
Oklahoma, Oklahoma
Oklahoma, OK U!
I'm a Sooner born and bred
And when I die, I'll be a Sooner dead
Rah Oklahoma, Rah Oklahoma
Rah Oklahoma, OK U!

The first University of Oklahoma student band was founded in 1904 by a freshman cornet player, Lloyd Curtis. The early all-male, 16-person band dressed in military-style uniforms and provided entertainment and created spirit at football games and other athletic events. The student band made its first trip to Stillwater, Oklahoma, for a game against Oklahoma A&M in 1913.

Women were first allowed into the band in the mid-1930s. And although times were tough during the Depression and World War II, the band continued to play at football games and other events.

The OU band received national televised coverage when it participated in the Orange Bowl and Orange Bowl Parade in Miami,

The Chant

Fans who wear the official colors—students, players, and alumni—are requested to stand and raise one finger in the air during the playing of the "Chant" at Oklahoma football games. It was written in 1936 by Jessie Lone Clarkson Gilkey, director of the Oklahoma women's glee club.

Our chant rolls on and on!
Thousands strong
Join heart and song
In alma mater's praise
Of campus beautiful by day and night
Of colors proudly gleaming Red and White
'Neath a western sky
OU's chant will never die.
Live on University!

"O.K. Oklahoma"

The fight song has been around since 1939 and has had different arrangements with different verses. It is played following touchdowns and when the Sooner Schooner comes on the field.

We'll march down the field with our heads held high,
Determined to win any battle we're in,
We'll fight with all our might for the Red and White.
March on, march on down the field for a victory is nigh.
You know we came to win the game for Oklahoma,
And so we will or know the reason why!
We'll march down the field with our heads held high,
With ev'ry resource we'll hold to the course,
And pledge our heart and soul to reach the goal.
March on, march on down the field as we sing the battle cry.
Dig in and fight for the Red and White of Oklahoma,
So we'll take home a victory or die!

Florida, in 1954, '56, '58, and '59. Earlier it got exposure performing at several Sugar Bowl games in New Orleans in 1949, 1950, and 1951.

The Pride of Oklahoma band has grown over the years, and is now more than 300 members strong. Over the decades the band has marched in its trademark formation: an interlocking *OU* while playing "Boomer Sooner." The song is also played at the end of each band rehearsal.

The other song the band plays often during football games is "Oklahoma!" the state song. The musical *Oklahoma!* debuted in 1943, at the height of World War II, and the song has become associated with OU football for decades.

76 Spy Game

"Will Rogers never met Barry Switzer."
—Darrell Royal, former Sooners player (1946–1949)
and Texas head coach (1957–1976)

The Oklahoma Sooners gave Texas coach Darrell Royal a rather rude sendoff in his final game at the Cotton Bowl. The game, a 6–6 tie, became known as the "Spy Game" and was one of the most brutal-hitting games in what was already a normally hard-hitting series between the two bitter border rivals.

Oklahoma had been tough on Royal in the 1970s, winning five straight from 1971 to 1975—a time period than included two OU head coaches, Chuck Fairbanks and Barry Switzer. In 1976 the Sooners were coming off back-to-back national championships and had squashed four straight opponents on the way to a No. 3 ranking nationally. Texas already had lost its season opener at Boston College 14–13 and was ranked 16th.

Shortly before the game at the Cotton Bowl in Dallas, Texas, Royal accused the Sooners of spying on the Longhorns' practices in Austin. Reporter Robert Heard quoted Royal as calling coach Barry Switzer and his assistant coaches "dirty bastards." Royal, a former Oklahoma Sooners football player, offered Switzer and the alleged spy, Lonnie Williams, $10,000 each if they could pass a polygraph test.

Previously, Williams had been a coach with OU defensive coordinator Larry Lacewell at Wichita State. Both Switzer and Lacewell denied the charges at the time. But years later Lacewell admitted to Royal that the spying accusations were true. However, no admissions were forthcoming before the game.

Just before the game started, Royal and Switzer walked down the tunnel with President Gerald Ford, who chatted with both coaches. But neither Royal nor Switzer spoke to each other, and both coaches were booed. It was that tense.

Texas held the upper hand and held a 6–0 lead deep into the fourth quarter, but with 5:23 remaining in the game, UT running back Ivey Suber fumbled at his own 37. Less than four minutes later, Oklahoma's Horace Ivory scored from the 1 to tie the game. With 1:38 remaining, it appeared that OU would snatch the victory. But a high snap followed. Oklahoma kicker Uwe von Schamann never got a chance to kick. He attempted a pass into the end zone that could have won the game, but it was intercepted by Texas' Steve Collier. The final score was 6–6.

Switzer said he felt as empty as UT did.

The tie did nothing for Texas the rest of the season, as the Longhorns finished 5–5–1 in Royal's last hurrah. Similarly, Oklahoma's season took a turn for the worse that year. Oklahoma lost two games in the middle of the season to Oklahoma State and

Colorado, and wound up in a three-way tie for the Big 8 title with those teams.

"We fought like hell for 60 minutes, and it came out a tie," Royal said afterward. "I don't feel like we won. I wouldn't be sitting here with my belly about to throw up again if I thought we had won."

And the 1976 tie to Texas also signaled a change in the tone of the series. Oklahoma lost five of the next seven games to Texas before tying them again in 1984.

77 Peter Gardere

Oklahoma had beaten Texas four straight times in the Red River Rivalry from 1985 to 1988 by an average score of 33–10. Entering the 1989 OU-Texas game, Sooners coach Gary Gibbs, in his first season, was hoping to continue the trend. And it appeared that Gibbs would when Oklahoma rallied from a 21–7 halftime deficit to take a 24–21 lead with just more than three minutes remaining in the game.

Enter Texas' redshirt freshman quarterback Peter Gardere, who started fashioning his legendary status. He completed four straight passes and took Texas to the OU 25-yard line. His fifth straight completion went to wide receiver Johnny Walker in the end zone with 1:33 remaining. UT won 28–24 to start a four-game Longhorns winning streak in the series.

"I went into the training room, and he [Gibbs] was sitting on the table and he had towel on him," said Donnie Duncan, who was the Oklahoma athletics director at the time. "He was wrung out. Gary Gibbs ran and kept in shape and everything, but he looked

OU's All-Conference Multiple Honors

There have been three players in Oklahoma football history who have been four-time all-conference selections, two nearly simultaneously in the mid-1980s. Tackle Wade Walker (1946–1949), defensive end Darrell Reed (1984–1987), and offensive guard Anthony Phillips (1985–1988).

extremely frail to me. His comment was, 'The football gods didn't smile on Oklahoma today.'"

And that was just the beginning. Gardere became OU's Public Enemy No. 1 in this storied series.

"The year before, I can remember Shannon Kelly [another UT quarterback] stopping me in the dorm and telling me that if you play or start in any game, make sure it is the OU game," said Gardere, who was then on the scout team. "And in the locker room, the whole week of the OU game the OU fight song is playing. You were so sick of it before the game. You were tired of hearing it."

In succeeding years, Gardere continued to break OU fans' hearts at the Cotton Bowl on the second Saturday of October each year and became the only quarterback in the history of the series to lead his team to four straight victories. He received the nickname "Peter the Great" for those performances.

The 1990 game had an equally painful ending for OU. Gardere authored another late comeback. Oklahoma had a No. 4 ranking coming into the game and had won five straight games by big margins that season. Yet Gardere shattered OU's dreams once again and sent them into a three-game tailspin with losses to Iowa State and Colorado the following two weeks.

Late in the game, with UT trailing 13–7, Gardere directed the Longhorns to the OU 16. And with two minutes remaining, he found Keith Cash in the end zone for the tying touchdown. The extra point gave Texas a 14–13 victory. "The Cash play was the exact same play we ran to Johnny Walker the year before," Gardere said.

Although Gardere didn't provide any late-game theatrics in the next two seasons, he started in both games and his team won: 10–7 in 1991 and 34–24 in 1992.

By the end of the 1992 game, Oklahoma fans directed a chant toward Gardere: "Graduate! Graduate!" Once he did, OU won the next game against Texas—38–17 in 1993—capturing Gibbs' only victory in the series during his six-year tenure.

78 Troy Aikman

Oklahoma was never known as a haven for great passers during the Barry Switzer era. In fact, until head coach Bob Stoops came to town in the late 1990s, passing was pretty much taboo in Norman. The fact that future All-Pro quarterback Troy Aikman, who led the Dallas Cowboys to three Super Bowl victories in 1992, '93, and '95, started at OU was probably due more to OU's proximity to his high school.

Gil Brandt, formerly vice president of player personnel for the Dallas Cowboys, remembers the first time he ever laid eyes on Troy Aikman. Mack Brown, then an assistant coach for Barry Switzer at Oklahoma, summoned the young Aikman to his office at Owen Field. Aikman was a rawboned youngster from tiny Henrietta, Oklahoma, during the 1984 season.

Future Texas coach Mack Brown had welcomed Aikman as a green freshman. This was long before Aikman would transfer to more pass-oriented UCLA, star there in 1987 and 1988, and become the Dallas Cowboys' top pick in 1989.

"Mack Brown was the offensive coordinator at OU when Aikman was a freshman," Brandt recalled of a 1984 episode. "I was in Mack's office looking at tape on an old Bell and Howell projector. Mack came in and said, 'We are going to start a new quarterback. I want you to meet him.' A few minutes later Aikman came into the office, and he was going to be the starting quarterback against Kansas. He said, 'I played for the He-he-henriet-ta-ta Hens.' The guy was nervous as all get out.

"Mack said, 'This guy is really going to be a good player.' I said, 'I hope he doesn't have to throw many passes this week.' He threw an interception that was returned for a touchdown [in KU's 28–11 victory]."

Aikman, who got the starting nod when Danny Bradley was injured, lettered as a freshman and as a sophomore (despite an injury), but elected to leave Switzer's ground-hog offense, which eventually would be led by Jamelle Holieway. He left for Los Angeles and coach Terry Donahue's passing attack at UCLA with two years of eligibility remaining. Aikman sat out the 1986 season and worked with Bruins assistant coach Rick Neuheisel, who would later be the head coach at Colorado, Washington, and UCLA, and is now a TV analyst.

In two seasons at UCLA, Aikman started all 24 games as the Bruins tied for first in the Pac-10 when he was a junior and finished second when he was a senior. Aikman completed 406 of 627 passes (64.8 percent) for 5,298 yards and 41 touchdowns. His completion percentage ranks second in UCLA history among players who have passed for at least 2,000 yards in their careers.

"Later, we worked out Aikman at UCLA. Jimmy [Johnson, who had become the new Cowboys coach] and I worked out Aikman. We got out to the practice field. He was throwing to people like you or me, managers or whatever. He threw 100 passes, and not one of them was uncatchable. Jimmy and I rode back to the airport, and Jimmy said, 'If we had him at Miami, we would have been 24–0 instead of 23–1 [in 1987 and 1988] and won every game by 50 points."

79 OU-Texas at the State Fair

There's nothing else like it. But if you can't get a ticket, at least stand outside and soak up the atmosphere at the State Fair of Texas.

On the second Saturday in early October the Oklahoma-Texas football game takes over the national college football spotlight. It's a must-see if you can snare a ticket—but it is not easy. Despite more than 92,000 seats, there's a waiting list at both schools that probably will never be diminished.

Inside the stadium, it is obvious why there's such a demand. The nearby clicking of rides and noise from the midway can be heard. The split stadium of 46,000 burnt orange–wearing fans in the north half of the bowl and 46,000 lunatics in crimson and cream in the south end is a spectacular sight. And two nationally ranked teams from border states where college football is high-stakes eyeball each other as they come out of the famous tunnel at the south end of the bowl.

"ESPN's *GameDay* says there is no other game like it because of the State Fair," said Errol McKoy, the just-retired State Fair of Texas president. "It makes it feel like a bowl game. It is splitting the stadium. It is people coming together in such a tradition. They may not have seen each other all year. All those things make it a special game. It is the perfect storm."

Just going to the State Fair of Texas on the day of the game is an experience, when the now 55-foot-high Big Tex, the talking cowboy, greets people at the fair's main entrance. And jumping on the dozens of amusement rides, including the 212-foot Texas Star's Ferris wheel, would take several days.

The Fair Park area is the year-round home of several museums and the Music Hall. Together, they form the largest collection of

Tasty Food to Enjoy at the State Fair of Texas

High-caloric food items available at the State Fair of Texas will be sure to keep you at the gym for an extended period of time. That is, if your arteries don't clog up before you leave Fair Park. Below is a list of food available during just one year. While the fried delights vary from fair to fair year to year, the emphasis is always on the fried and decadent.

Chicken-fried bacon—Thick and peppery Farm Pac® bacon is seasoned, double-dipped in a special batter and breading, and deep-fried. Served with a creamy side of ranch or honey-mustard sauce.

Fried banana split—A mixture of banana and honey peanut butter is rolled in balls, battered and deep-fried, and topped with assorted, delicious fixings, including powdered sugar, caramel and chocolate syrups, chopped peanuts, whipped cream, and banana-split-flavored ice cream bites, then fittingly crowned with the traditional cherry.

Texas-fried Jelly Belly beans—Jelly Belly beans are rolled in funnel cake batter and fried to a crunch. People can share the treat with friends and try to guess the flavors before biting down.

Fried chocolate truffles—A silky-smooth, handmade, dark chocolate truffle is rolled in cocoa powder before being battered and deep-fried. The melting chocolate goodness is dusted in cinnamon, sugar, and cocoa powder.

Chocolate-covered strawberry waffle balls—Plump fresh strawberries covered in a thick chocolate shell are dipped in a sweet, waffle batter and deep-fried. Dusted with powdered sugar and served on a stick.

Green bean fries—Fresh green beans lightly battered, deep fried, and served with a side of cucumber ranch dressing for dipping!

Jalapeno deep-fried gorditas—Jalapeno-flavored gorditas are cooked on the grill and then deep fried, stuffed with beef, chicken, or beans and cheese, and finally topped with lettuce, tomato, guacamole, and more cheese.

Ignited Moon Pie—The Original Moon Pie, lightly battered and deep fried, then gently sprinkled with powdered sugar!

From: The State Fair of Texas website listings of food

*A food locator is available when you get to the State Fair of Texas. There are approximately 200 food service locations in the 277-acre entertainment and recreational complex.

art deco exposition buildings in the United States. Much of the 37,000 square feet of exhibition space in Fair Park is used during the fair's 24-day run. There are various craft, food, and livestock competitions, as well as automobile shows and other products being demonstrated. Frequent concerts by well-known artists are also a part of the entertainment. And don't forget the food. The State Fair of Texas is the place where corn dogs were first served in 1942 and turkey drumsticks abound. Plus there's an array of other food to enjoy.

"The State Fair is an astounding addition to the game," said Donnie Duncan, a former OU assistant coach, Sooners athletics director, and former Big 12 Conference associate commissioner of the entire game experience. "As far as I am concerned, it is a treasure in sports that cannot be duplicated."

80 Eddie Crowder

In 1951 and 1952 Eddie Crowder, coming out of Muskogee, Oklahoma, ended up becoming the leader as quarterback, bridging Bud Wilkinson's great teams from 1948 to 1950 and the beginning of the 47-game winning streak in 1953. Smart and feisty, he also was a standout safety for Wilkinson, who would spot him there at times.

Years later, when Crowder was head coach of Colorado from 1963 to 1973, he said, "I've only known one genius in my lifetime. It was Bud Wilkinson."

"Bud had such effect on these guys," said National Football Foundation executive director Steve Hatchell, who was a Colorado team manager. "Eddie was from Muskogee.... He had sort of adopted the mannerisms of Bud Wilkinson. He wouldn't say 'defense.' He would call it 'de-fence.' We got to be better on 'de-fence.' When they were standing side-by-side and they were talking, you could see how a young guy coming in from Muskogee could be affected by a guy like Bud Wilkinson."

In 1952, Crowder's senior year, Oklahoma led the country in scoring (40.7 points a game) but failed to compete for the national championship: an opening-season 21–21 tie at Colorado and a 27–21 loss at Notre Dame held them back. The Sooners finished No. 4 in both major polls, with Crowder at quarterback, Billy Vessels at left halfback, Buck McPhail at fullback, and Buddy Leake at right halfback. Leake, a highly recruited player out of Memphis, was a just a sophomore. Crowder, Vessels, and McPhail, all seniors, were All-Americans that season.

McPhail, who was the main blocking back for Vessels, the 1952 Heisman Trophy winner, still rushed for 1,018 yards. Vessels had 1,072 yards and 17 touchdowns to become Oklahoma's first Heisman Trophy winner. And Crowder ran the show for the Sooners, who won the Big 7 with a 5–0–1 record.

"Eddie was an excellent ball-handler and a heck of a leader," said OU guard J.D. Roberts, the 1953 Outland Trophy winner. "He was one of the best ball handlers I had ever been around. He was an adequate passer, but a real leader. And when we played against somebody who was giving us problems in our secondary, Crowder went in at safety."

Later Crowder was selected in the second round of the 1953 NFL Draft by the New York Giants, but he never played for the team because of a nerve injury in his throwing arm. His future was in coaching. He spent seven seasons as Wilkinson's assistant, from 1956 to 1962, after spending a season at Army as an assistant. And he took part of Wilkinson with him in his pregame routines and preparations. Crowder would get his quarterbacks out on the field on the Friday walkthrough.

Eddie Crowder, who played quarterback on the great Oklahoma teams in the early 1950s, compiled a record of 67–49–2 in 11 seasons as Colorado's coach, from 1963 to 1973. He also served as athletics director starting in 1965, a role he continued in until 1984.

"Eddie went through this with Bud," Hatchell said. "You would go down to the field and you would be standing on your 22-yard line and 78 yards to go for a touchdown. And Eddie would say, 'It is third-and-eight, what are we going to call?' Then you go to the other hash mark, and it is first-and-10. And you would do this up and down the field, so if you had this end zone or that end zone, do that an hour and a half. Bud would do all of that. Here is why we are doing that. Here are the circumstances you are going to be in."

At Colorado from 1963 to 1973, Crowder compiled a 67–49–2 record, and his teams went to five bowls. The high point came in the 1971 season, when Colorado finished third in the Associated Press poll behind Nebraska and Oklahoma, two other Big 8 teams. After he retired from coaching, he became the school's athletics director. Crowder was inducted into the Oklahoma Sports Hall of Fame in 2003. He passed away in 2008 at age 77.

81 Walter "Waddy" Young

More than 70 years later, the Walter "Waddy" Young Squadron, Cadets from the Air Force ROTC Detachment on the University of Oklahoma campus, still recognize one of the Sooners' most inspirational and talented players. A World War II hero, Young was a standout end in the late 1930s.

The 6', 203-pounder, an All-Stater at Ponca City High School, was one of the main stars on the Sooners' first bowl team that allowed only 12 points during the regular season. The Sooners finished the regular season with a 10–0 mark and had a 14-game winning streak before losing to Tennessee 17–0 in the Orange Bowl.

He was All-Big 6 as a junior in 1937 as well as in 1938, when he became the Sooners' first consensus All-American—selected to three different All-America teams at the time. He was equally good as a receiver or a defensive cover man for coach Tom Stidham's 1938 Big 6 champions.

The Sooners upset Rice 7–6 in the first game of the 1938 season and allowed only Tulsa to score the rest of the regular season. Young was a great blocker in Stidham's single- and double-wing offenses. He was tough—a top wrestler for the Sooners and the University of Oklahoma's heavyweight boxing champion.

But maybe more importantly, he was a leader—on the field and as a squadron commander in World War II. "When you met Waddy, you could tell right away he was a leader," said Barth Walker, a Sooners lineman from 1935 to 1937. "'His teammates looked up to him, and he had great respect. He always carried himself well, and that showed on the football field and in life."

Young was drafted by the Brooklyn Dodgers football team in the third round and played two seasons professionally before joining the Army Air Corps near the end of 1940. He entered flight training in early 1941 and received his wings in August of that year. Flying between Newfoundland and England, Young had 9,000 combat hours, all in a B-24 Liberator. He shot down two Nazi fighter planes and attacked a Nazi submarine during that tour of duty. Young was awarded the first Oak Leaf Cluster for the Air Medal of Distinguished Service.

Switching to the Pacific Theater in 1944, Young became a squadron commander and was assigned a B-29. His Woody's Wagon was at the front of a formation that first bombed Tokyo in November 1944. But Young's plane was shot down on January 9, 1945, when, heading back to his Saipan base after completing a bombing mission, he circled back to help a friend in another plane that was losing speed and altitude. Both planes were shot down over the Sea of Japan.

In 1960 a honorary group of ROTC students designated their organization the Walter "Waddy" Young Squadron. In 1986 he was inducted into the College Football Hall of Fame, and in 2007 Young was inducted into the Oklahoma Sports Hall of Fame. He also was awarded the Bob Kalsu Freedom Award, given to an individual who has made extraordinary personal contributions and/or sacrifices.

82 Harold Keith

There's a plaque with a bronzed likeness of Harold Keith in the football press box at the University of Oklahoma. It's fitting because he once designed the previous Owen Field press box in 1951, which is why the much newer one is named after him.

Mr. Keith, who passed away in 1998 in his mid-nineties, simply became a legend at the University of Oklahoma, laying the blueprint for the modern-day sports information director and serving as the front man for Bud Wilkinson's juggernaut program in the 1950s. His award-winning career culminated in 1987, when he was inducted into the Oklahoma Sports Hall of Fame.

"He was way ahead of his time," said College Football Playoff Executive Director Bill Hancock, who knew Mr. Keith, as he was called, and worked in the OU SID office in the 1970s as a student. "He was a writer himself, so he knew what they needed. He took care of national and local press almost better than anybody in the country. He was among the first half-dozen SIDs. He went to the school in the late '20s and ran cross-country."

Mr. Keith worked at the *Hutchinson* (Kansas) *News*, became the University of Oklahoma's first SID in 1930, and held that

Did You Know?
Jack Mitchell, OU's quarterback in 1948, was tired of getting tackled carrying the ball during the annual grudge match against Texas. So before he got tackled, he would pitch it, and the halfback would pick up yardage. This worked in a 20–14 victory over the Longhorns. OU coach Bud Wilkinson got the idea to continue the practice—the option.

post until 1969. He served during tenures of 10 Oklahoma football coaches before he retired, but his experiences with Wilkinson were what made him famous across the country. He later authored several books, including *47 Straight*, a compilation of 61 interviews with Wilkinson's players during that era, from 1953 to 1957.

"He talked about the boys.... Bud's boys were so talented, the shy ones were so shy," Hancock said. "He wrote feature stories about them. He wrote some remarkable features. He would interview them and find out about their families, like the Scotch-Irish halfback from Muskogee.... It showed a reporter's skill and how a writer's heart helped him do his job. He was gentle."

The late Mr. Keith, in an interview with the *Daily Oklahoman*, revealed how he learned some of his trade from Oklahoma football coach Lawrence "Biff" Jones (1935–1936). "He was only here for two years in the 1930s, but coach Biff Jones taught me more about publicity than anybody I ever worked for," Mr. Keith told the newspaper. "I thought only in terms of local publicity. Jones had been at Army at one time and had this big rivalry with [Knute] Rockne. He was acquainted with all the great columnists and put me in touch with them."

Mr. Keith basically was a one-man operation early on in his career. He put together a Sooners football program for home games and wrote a weekly sports newsletter—and he printed it, folded it, and took it to the post office himself, according to his sketch at the Oklahoma Sports Hall of Fame.

"You never saw him get excited," Hancock added. "He was always teaching. And he was a fabulous archivist. We had files in the early 1970s of OU sporting events that happened in the early 1930s. I am sure those files are still there. He would write on 3 x 5 cards, the tiniest cards, about 1938 cross-country and 1940 golf."

Mr. Keith won the Helms Foundation Award as the top SID in the country in 1950. He was president of CoSIDA (College Sports Information Directors) in 1964 and 1965. And in 1987 he was a recipient of the University of Oklahoma's Distinguished Service Citation.

83 Bob's Steak & Chop House

Former coach Barry Switzer might be seen on the eve of the annual Oklahoma-Texas game sitting on a bar stool—well, just briefly—and then dining at the original Bob's Steak & Chop House on Lemmon Avenue.

Switzer has been a staple at Bob's on Lemmon since he was coach of the Dallas Cowboys, a be-seen place for Dallas sports types such as Jerry Jones, Troy Aikman, Mike Modano, and even Oklahoma State's main sports benefactor, T. Boone Pickens of oil and gas fame.

The original owner, Bob Sambol, became good friends with Switzer.

During the 2008 season, when Sambol attended a Norman gathering of players from the Oklahoma and Nebraska 1971 Game of the Century—won 35–31 by Nebraska—Switzer was at the podium and addressing the crowd of players and assistant coaches.

Suddenly, the unpredictable Switzer spotted his friend Bob in the crowd: "And any time you are in Dallas, make sure you go to Bob's, it's the best steak house in Dallas!"

"It was like a commercial," Sambol said, with a grin.

Sambol elected to close the restaurant on the eve of the 2007 Oklahoma-Texas game when the restaurant could have made $50,000 that night. It was Switzer's 70th birthday. Sambol's incentive was as a friend, although Switzer's daughter Kathy and good friend country-western singer Toby Keith and other friends contributed money to close the place.

According to a story in the *Dallas Morning News*, Bob was part of the cover for the surprise party, telling Barry he could come by and have a drink, but a private party was occupying all the dining rooms. Little did Barry know, the private party, attended by a couple hundred people, was for him. Lots of well-known personalities and former players attended, such as quarterback Dean Blevins and Dallas Cowboys owner Jerry Jones, one of Barry's former teammates at Arkansas and his employer when Barry was coach of the Cowboys.

Dave Sittler, a highly respected columnist for the *Tulsa World*, was invited to the surprise party. He went out to a late dinner but still had time to take another buddy to Bob's for Barry's surprise party. Sure enough, there was Barry on the stool, spinning stories into the early morning.

In his trips to Dallas, Barry usually makes it to Bob's. Check with the front to see if he's there—he might be in one of the booths.

84 Quarterback Shuffle

The 2013 season presented one of the more interesting quarterback rotations in Sooner history after senior Landry Jones had departed. Freshman redshirt quarterback Trevor Knight won the right to start the season opener against Louisiana-Monroe. And junior quarterback Blake Bell, the "Belldozer," began the 2013 season on the bench, a familiar position in his first two seasons.

"We thought we had the guy in Trevor," said Oklahoma co-offensive coordinator Josh Heupel of Knight, a four-star recruit who won the 2013 preseason competition. "Trevor gets dinged, injured [against West Virginia in the second game]. Blake comes in and plays well. He gets dinged up [Iowa State, 10th game]. Trevor goes in and continues to compete and plays well. For four years we had Landry who didn't get hurt in a single ballgame.

"Our players believe in both of those guys. They really believe and have a lot of confidence in those guys that they're going to go out and play at a high level," Heupel added. "For me personally, I have enjoyed it, because there is great competition inside the room…It has been fun how we have been able to change through-out the course of the season—with all the injuries that we had and with all the different personnel changes that we've had."

In the second game of the season, a 16–7 victory against West Virginia, Knight suffered a bruised knee. That gave way for the 6'6" 263-pound Bell, the short-yard specialist off the bench his first two seasons behind Jones, for his initial career start the next game against Tulsa.

Bell responded with an eye-popping 413 yards passing and four touchdowns in a 51–20 victory. Those were the most passing yards for a first-game starting quarterback in OU history, surpassing

Sam Bradford's 363 yards against North Texas in 2007. Oklahoma coach Bob Stoops named Bell the starter for the Notre Dame game, which Oklahoma won 35–21 two weeks later.

Bell wound up starting eight of 13 games, but lost the starting job for good after suffering a concussion in the 10th game of the season against Iowa State. Then Knight came back in to start as the Sooners beat Kansas State, Oklahoma State, and finally Alabama in the Sugar Bowl. Bell was needed in a strong backup role in the second half of the 33–24 victory in Stillwater after Knight separated his non-throwing shoulder in the first half.

"We continued to help each other grow and we've always been ready to play," Knight said of the dual quarterback system. "The Oklahoma State game, for instance, all three of us [including sophomore Kendal Thompson] had to play. It's just about coming into each game ready to be the guy that day. You can either butt heads or come together and make each other better, and I feel like we've come together this year."

Knight recovered from the shoulder problem, started against Alabama, and put together a career game against the Tide. He had personal collegiate passing bests in completions (32), yards (348), and touchdowns (four). Knight's completions were the most in Sugar Bowl history. His passing touchdowns tied a Sugar Bowl record and set an Oklahoma bowl record.

Going into the 2014 season, Knight is the OU starter. Bell has moved to tight end.

"The more snaps you get, the more comfortable you feel," Knight said after the Sugar Bowl. "The more completions you get, the more comfortable you feel. And it's all about getting in that rhythm, hitting a few shots early, set the rhythm, the tone for the game. The more snaps you get, the more comfortable you are. Moving forward from that, going into next year, that's what we're going to ride on."

85 Transition Years

One of the stranger seasons in Oklahoma history was 1995, which ended with a flat record of 5–5–1. The Sooners exchanged head coaches, going from the conservative Gibbs to the bombastic Howard Schnellenberger. Sooners fans didn't know how good they had it with Gibbs (44–23–2), who resigned late in the 1994 season but was allowed to coach until the season's end.

Schnellenberger, who had resurrected Miami's program in the 1980s and made Louisville a respectable team before arriving in Norman, made his presence felt before he even stepped on the field.

Sitting in the press box during Gibbs' last game, a 31–6 loss to BYU in the Copper Bowl, Schnellenberger criticized players for being "out of shape, unorganized, and unmotivated." He also proclaimed that he would become famous by the time he left the state and that movies and books would be written about him.

Before the 1995 season, his driver and PR man, Ron Steiner, had escorted Schnellenberger to the *Dallas Morning News* for a meeting and goodwill mission with influential executive sports editor Dave Smith. To say OU's relationship had been chilly with the *News* under the regime of Barry Switzer was an understatement. Gibbs just served out the probation and kept his mouth shut.

Schnellenberger certainly knew he needed all the good publicity he could get—and what better way than to play up to one of the country's top newspapers.

A few years before, Switzer had become so enraged over a story the *Dallas Morning News* had written about alleged ticket improprieties with Sooners players during the 1980s, he publicly threatened to ask Sooners officials that the Oklahoma-Texas game be moved out of the Cotton Bowl in Dallas. "It was the Dallas press," Switzer

Billy Sims' Breakout Game

In 1978, on the day Oklahoma played Texas, Billy Sims was calm on the bus ride from the team hotel in Fort Worth to the Cotton Bowl. Sims, a highly celebrated recruit from Hooks, Texas, had redshirted in 1976 because of an injury and really hadn't proven himself during the 1977 season. By 1978 he was poised to show what he could do. He won the Heisman Trophy that year.

"Gary Gibbs had graduated and he was a graduate assistant coach, and he is sitting next to Billy on the bus," said Donnie Duncan, OU's running backs coach at the time. "So Billy had been under wraps. The Texas media said, 'He shouldn't have gone there and where is Billy Sims?' And Gibbs asked, 'Billy, are you nervous?' And Billy said, 'No, Coach.' And Gibbs said, 'Why aren't you nervous? Everybody else on this bus is nervous.' And Sims said, 'I know what I am going to do, Coach.'"

said in the early 1990s. "They treated us like a bastard son. We came down there, and it wasn't neutral. It never will be. It was rehash of my deal or something negative every year.... We got tired of that." It turned out to be an idle threat, but nevertheless demonstrated his anger.

In order to restore some civility to the relationship with the Dallas media, Schnellenberger talked a good game, even if the meeting with the *News* was rather superficial and predictably overly optimistic about the season's prospects. The Sooners did start 3–0 in 1995, but the team finished 2–5–1 and posted its first losing record in conference play in 30 years. Schnellenberger lost to Oklahoma State, the Sooners' first loss to the Cowboys since 1976.

One peculiar incident occurred before the Sooners' 13–9 victory over Missouri in Columbia—Schnellenberger's last win as a Sooners coach. While some news media drove down to the game, a radio report announced that Schnellenberger had taken his team into Missouri and stopped off to tour a winery between Kansas City and Columbia. OU officials confirmed the incident. Jokes were flowing as to what the coach was doing while his Sooners went on the tour.

Oklahoma sources have indicated that Schnellenberger's removal as Oklahoma coach after one season had much to do with his private disagreements with Oklahoma president David Boren over running the football program.

"Howard's methods work," said Donnie Duncan, who was the OU athletics director when Schnellenberger was hired. "Some of his methods didn't fit [at Oklahoma].... There's a long story there.... He is a damn good football coach."

Schnellenberger later became head coach of Florida Atlantic and ushered that program into major-college football before retiring following the 2011 season.

In 1996 John Blake took over the OU head coaching spot at the strong urging of Switzer, who had worked with Blake while Switzer was head coach of the Dallas Cowboys. The hire also was perceived as a good move by Oklahoma in light of the call for minority head coaches in college football.

"Everybody seemed to think it was a really good idea at that particular point and time," said Duncan.

Blake, an Oklahoma graduate and former assistant coach for the Sooners, was an excellent recruiter. In fact, some of that leftover talent from his regime helped lay the foundation for Bob Stoops' national title in 2000. But Blake was a disastrous head coach, lowering the ceiling of expectations at OU with records of 3–8, 4–8, and 5–6 from 1996 to 1998. It was the first time since 1922 through 1924 that OU had posted three straight losing seasons.

Since his head-coaching days at OU, Blake has held assistant coaching positions at Mississippi State, Nebraska, and North Carolina, but now is out of coaching after a three-year NCAA show-cause penalty (in 2012) for violations while with the Tar Heels.

86 Port Robertson

Port Robertson was the University of Oklahoma wrestling coach for 14 years, from 1947 to 1959 and again in 1962, and was the disciplinarian for the Oklahoma football team for many more years than that. He once famously said, "Though our problems may be varied and many, if we don't beat Texas, we won't have any."

The late Robertson, a former All-America wrestler who passed away in 2003, was a bottom-line guy and not always popular with Oklahoma football players. But for three decades, until he retired in the mid-1980s, he handled discipline issues. He was an assistant athletics director and, at one time, the freshman football coach. He also was the athletics department's academic representative on the OU faculty and an academic counselor.

He turned what was a non-scholarship program after World War II into a national power and led OU to three national wrestling titles in the 1950s. He also ran the "O" Club, made up of the University of Oklahoma alumni sports letter-winners, until his retirement. A wrestling center on campus has been named after him, and he was inducted into the Oklahoma Sports Hall of Fame in 1995 as a wrestling coach.

It wasn't unusual during his early years an athletics enforcer for Robertson to have players in any sport running the steps at Memorial Stadium as a consequence of some transgression.

Frank Wolfson, an OU swimmer in the 1970s, remembers chuckling with his buddy Willie Franklin, a wide receiver on the football team in 1970 and 1971, about being called "Pea Heads" by Robertson for violating a rule. Wolfson and Franklin weren't the only athletes who were "lucky" enough to earn the distinction.

"Anyone who crossed paths with Port had a story," said Wolfson, who now runs a successful dentistry practice in Overland Park, Kansas. "He ran the athletic dorm and he had rules. He basically had it locked down there at night. And you had to be up and out by 8:00 AM from your room with your bed made. If not, you were sent to Port's office. And you didn't want that."

All the athletes, including the football players, had curfews, and females were not allowed above the reception and lounge area on the first floor.

Wolfson failed to make his bed by the prescribed time one day and was sent to Port's office. He was called a "Pea Head" and received a week of washing dishes in the jock dorm.

"He was more intimidating than anything," Wolfson said. "He was gruff. He was not real tall, but he was very thick and had a round head and short, cropped hair. He had big arms and thick arms, and you would say, 'Yes, sir.'"

87 Bob Kalsu

One of the highest honors an Oklahoma football player can receive is the Bob Kalsu Award, which is annually given to a player who demonstrates "uncommon dedication and fortitude." Oklahoma fans can learn more about Kalsu by going to the Armory just north of Memorial Stadium.

There, at the entrance, the late Kalsu, a former OU All-America offensive tackle in 1967, is memorialized in a ROTC tribute. It in includes his portrait, along with depictions of the Sooners, Buffalo Bills, and his military background. Below the portrait, there's a framed *Sports Illustrated* story about Kalsu's life, which ended on July 21, 1970. He became the only active professional football player to die in Vietnam when he was overcome by North Vietnamese mortar fire.

Kalsu was recruited out of Del City, Oklahoma, and had four different OU head coaches—Bud Wilkinson, Gomer Jones, Jim Mackenzie, and Chuck Fairbanks. In his senior season of 1967, Kalsu was named an All-American on the 10–1 Big 8 championship team that defeated Tennessee 26–24 in the Orange Bowl.

"Bob was our best offensive lineman, the best athlete we had," said Barry Switzer, who was an Oklahoma assistant from 1966 to 1972 before becoming head coach. "Bob wasn't only a great player, he was a great leader. He had the maturity and leadership abilities we needed at that time with our program in transition."

Kalsu, a member of ROTC at OU, graduated in May 1968 with a degree in education and was commissioned as a second lieutenant in the U.S. Army, but he was not immediately called up to serve. The Bills drafted him in the eighth round of the AFL-NFL draft. Kalsu became a starter for the Bills but would play only one season of professional football.

He was called up to join the U.S. Army's 101st Airborne Division and fulfilled his military obligations by going to Vietnam. He was living in Firebase Ripcord, an isolated jungle mountaintop and was giving artillery support to the infantry of the 101st Airborne when he was killed. Kalsu left behind his wife, Jan Darrow, whom he married shortly after he played his final college game at Oklahoma, his 20-month-old daughter, and a son who was born just two days after his death.

Kalsu's likeness can be seen in several areas on the OU campus. His name is engraved on the OU Stadium's War Memorial, the Army ROTC's Wall of Fame in Norman, the Buffalo Bill's Wall of Fame, and the Vietnam Memorial in Washington, D.C. In 1978 a plaque honoring his heroism was given to the Pro Football Hall of Fame by the Buffalo Bills. The plaque reads: "No one will ever know how great a football player Bob might have been, but we do know how great a man he was to give up his life for his country."

In May 2003 he was recognized in Iraq when Forward Operating Base Kalsu was established by the 105th Military Police Company, an Army National Guard unit from Buffalo, New York. The U.S. Military installation in Iraq is located in Iskandariya, 20 miles south of Baghdad.

88 OU's Cradle of Coaches

Several of Bud Wilkinson's players from the 1940s and 1950s developed into future head coaches. Many of them were returning from military duty during World War II. The players were older and hardened by years of fighting and serving their country overseas, and college football served as a way to get back into civilian life.

Wilkinson had come to Oklahoma with head coach Jim Tatum as a package deal in 1946. Tatum had previously coached at North Carolina for one season in 1942, before enlisting in the navy during World War II. He was assigned to the Iowa Pre-Flight School, where he was line coach and assisted coach Don Faurot, who had developed the split-T offense in the early 1940s at Missouri. Wilkinson also was at Iowa Pre-Flight as a backfield coach.

After World War II, Faurot left the Pre-Flight School and went back to coach at Missouri. Following the war, in 1946, Tatum coached at Oklahoma before he was lured to Maryland by a big financial package, leaving the more popular Wilkinson as the logical choice to become the Sooners' head coach.

Running principally the same split-T offense, Wilkinson was fortunate to get better players at Oklahoma than Faurot did at Missouri and began winning big immediately in Norman. Oklahoma would dominate the Midlands for 15 years. Tatum also used the split-T at Maryland in 1953 to win the national title, although Oklahoma did beat the Terrapins in the Orange Bowl the season after they were crowned national champions.

Wilkinson's Oklahoma players were well-suited to the split-T offense and all had keen football minds, which they demonstrated when they later wound up on the sideline as head coaches:

Jim Owens (1946–1949, OU end from Oklahoma City, Oklahoma): Owens was head coach of University of Washington Huskies from 1957 to 1974 and had back-to-back Rose Bowl triumphs over Big Ten teams Wisconsin and Minnesota. His overall record in Seattle was 99–82–6.

Darrell Royal (1946–1949, OU quarterback, punter from Hollis, Oklahoma): Royal was head coach of Mississippi State for 1954 and 1955 and the Washington Huskies for 1956 before going to the University of Texas, where he was head coach from 1957 to 1976 and compiled a 167–47–5 record. He won three national titles and 11 SWC titles, went to 16 bowl games, and had 11 top 10 finishes with the Longhorns.

Dee Andros (1946–1949, OU lineman from Oklahoma City, Oklahoma): The "Great Pumpkin" was head coach at Idaho (1962–1964) and at Oregon State (1965–1975). His brother Plato was an All-America lineman at OU in 1946. Oregon State's 3–0 upset of top-ranked USC in 1967 ranks as the high point of his coaching tenure at Oregon State. He had a 51–64–1 overall record at Oregon State. He beat rival Oregon nine times in 11 tries.

Bert Clark (1949–1951, OU linebacker from Wichita Falls, Texas): Clark was Washington State's head coach from 1964 to 1967 and had a 15–24–1 record. The 1965 Cougars were known as the "Cardiac Kids" because they rallied to win several games in the final minutes or seconds, including three against Big Ten teams on the road.

Wade Walker (1946–1949, OU tackle from Gastonia, North Carolina): Walker was Mississippi State's head coach from 1956 to 1961 and succeeded Darrell Royal, his OU teammate, as head coach of the Bulldogs. Walker, who later returned to Oklahoma as athletics director, had only one winning season in Starkville, 6–2–1 in 1957.

Jack Mitchell (1946–1948, OU quarterback from Arkansas City, Kansas): Mitchell was head coach at Wichita State (1953–1954) with a 13–5–1 record, at Arkansas (1955–1957) with a 17–12–1 mark, and finally at Kansas (1958–1966) with 44–42–5 record. His 1961 Jayhawks (7–3–1) beat Rice 33–7 in the Bluebonnet Bowl. Running back Gale Sayers was on his team from 1962 to 1964, but the Jayhawks failed to go to a bowl during that time.

Pete Tillman (1946–1948, OU center from Mangum, Oklahoma): Tillman was Wichita State's head coach in 1955 and 1956 and posted a 11–8–1 record in his two seasons there.

Warren Giese (1946, OU end): Giese was South Carolina's head coach from 1956 to 1960 and posted a 28–21–1 overall record. His high points were two 7–3 records in 1956 and 1958.

Eddie Crowder (1950–1952, OU quarterback from Muskogee, Oklahoma): Crowder was coach of Colorado from 1963 to 1973 and the school's athletics director until 1984. He compiled a 67–49–2 record, and his teams went to five bowls. The high point was the 1971 season, when Colorado finished third in the Associated Press poll behind Nebraska and Oklahoma, two other Big 8 teams.

89 Oklahoma's Lost Gator Bowl

"Maybe I will get my reward in heaven."
—Oklahoma coach Gomer Jones after declaring
four OU players ineligible prior to the January 2,
1965, Gator Bowl against Florida State

Gil Brandt vividly recalls the events in December 1964 when he was pursuing Oklahoma All-America tackle Ralph Neely, who wound up playing 13 seasons for the Cowboys from 1965 to 1977 and played in four Super Bowls.

"The Baltimore Colts drafted him, but they couldn't sign him," said Brandt, who was the Dallas Cowboys' director of player personnel at the time. "Oklahoma was playing in the Gator Bowl. And on December 12 they give us the rights to Neely. I took a flight to Oklahoma City and drove down to Norman and to the married housing area. I got there, and Neely was at practice. Diane Forte was his wife, and she was showing me their wedding pictures. About 5:30, Ralph walked in, and I said, 'I guess you know we have got your [NFL] rights from the Colts.' He said, 'To be honest with you, I already signed with the Oilers.'"

Indeed, court records later indicated Neely had received a $25,000 signing bonus from the Oilers of the AFL and owner Bud Adams. In addition, he had been promised a job at a real estate firm and interest in a service station. Of course, this was against NCAA rules and would ultimately lead to Neely being declared ineligible for the Sooners' Gator Bowl game against Florida State.

Three other Sooners offensive players—fullback Jim Grisham, halfback Lance Rentzel, and reserve end Wes Skidgel—also had signed contracts with professional teams and were declared ineligible by Oklahoma head coach Gomer Jones prior to the game. Without three key offensive starters, Oklahoma lost 36–19. The Sooners managed only 71 yards rushing, while Florida State had 520 yards of total offense.

Brandt had been led to believe by Cowboys officials who had ties with the Sooners that negotiations with Neely would be easy. But they weren't. Brandt also had to deal with Neely's father-in-law, Bob Forte, who was acting as a go-between. In order to sweeten the pot and lure Neely away from the rival AFL Oilers, Brandt invited Forte down for a Cowboys game in Dallas. Forte told Brandt he would have dinner on his own after the game. "I called Arthur's [a fashionable Dallas restaurant] and told them he was coming and to send me the bill," Brandt recalled. "A week later I got a bill, and it was for, like, $800. Back then that was about, like, $10,000."

As things progressed, Neely decided on the Cowboys over the Oilers, although he still had the signed contract with Oilers owner Bud Adams. Brandt told Forte to go to the Gator Bowl and he would put him up at the beachside Ponte Verde Resort. Neely could then sign legally with the Cowboys after the game back in Dallas. Neely tried to return the bonus. Before OU's January 2 Gator Bowl in Jacksonville, Florida, Neely disclosed to Jones what was going on and was declared ineligible for the game.

"It's New Year's Day, 12:00 at night," Brandt recalled, "and Coach Landry called me and asked, 'What did you do?' Gomer Jones called me and said Neely was declared ineligible because he signed with the Cowboys. I told him I did not sign the guy."

After much fanfare and a lawsuit filed by the Oilers against Neely to get their rights to him back, Dallas gave up draft picks to the Oilers and was forced to play three preseason games in Houston. But Neely came to Dallas and starred.

90 Developing Linemen

Gomer Jones was the architect of Bud Wilkinson's lines every step of the way during Wilkinson's tenure from 1947 to 1963. Jones developed 16 interior linemen who were All-Americans during that period before he succeeded Wilkinson as coach. He then developed two more during his brief tenure as OU's head coach in 1964 and 1965.

Jones, who played high school football at East High in Cleveland, Ohio, was a consensus All-America center at Ohio State in 1935 and team captain. He later was an assistant coach at Ohio

All-America Linemen Developed by Gomer Jones

Buddy Burris (Guard) 1946–1948
Wade Walker (Tackle) 1949
Stanley West (Guard) 1949
*Jim Weatherall (Tackle) 1950–1951
Tom Catlin (Center) 1951–1952
*J.D. Roberts (Guard) 1953
Kurt Burris (Center) 1954
Bo Bolinger (Guard) 1955
Ed Gray (Guard) 1956
Bill Krisher (Guard) 1956–1957
Jerry Tubbs (Center) 1956
Bob Harrison (Center) 1958
Jerry Thompson (Guard) 1959
Leon Cross (Guard) 1962
Ralph Neely (Tackle) 1963–1964
Wayne Lee (Center) 1962
+Carl McAdams (Center) 1964
+Granville Liggins (Nose guard) 1966–1967

*Outland Trophy Winner
+Jones was head coach in 1964 and 1965, but he developed Liggins.

State, John Carroll University, St. Mary's Pre-Flight School, and at Nebraska before joining Wilkinson at Oklahoma in 1947, when Wilkinson became head coach of the Sooners.

"I saw a film of him [and Ohio State] playing Notre Dame in either 1934 or 1935," said J.D. Roberts, one of two Outland Trophy winners who Jones developed at Oklahoma. "He gave it to me and some of the other players to watch. He was one heck of a player. And he did a heck of a job with the centers at Oklahoma."

Jones developed All-America centers at Oklahoma in the 1950s, like Barry Switzer did running backs two decades later during another OU dynasty. With Jones teaching technique and

Oklahoma coach Bud Wilkinson (left) and assistant coach Gomer Jones are shown on the sideline during a November 1949 game in Norman.

the repetitions the Sooners had under Wilkinson's carefully developed practice plans, the centers were precision-like in the running game.

"We were running teams, the split-T," Roberts said. "And what passing we did was play-action."

From 1951 to 1958, Oklahoma had four All-America centers: Tom Catlin (1951 and 1952) from Ponca City; Kurt Burris (1954) from Muskogee; Jerry Tubbs from Breckenridge, Texas (1956); and Bob Harrison from Stamford, Texas (1958). Harry Moore was a standout OU center in 1950 after returning from military duty, but made only All–Big 7. The four All-America centers then played linebacker on defense.

91 OU's Great Two-Way Players

Ralph Neely (Tackle) 1962–64; All-America 1963, 1964: An excellent blocker, Neely sprang holes for backs Jim Grisham and Joe Don Looney. Missouri quarterback Gary Lane said after a 13–3 OU victory in 1963, "I think he spent more time in our backfield than I did." He later became a star lineman for the Dallas Cowboys.

Joe Don Looney (Halfback, Punter) 1962–63; All-America 1962: Looney led the Sooners in rushing in only one season, with 852 yards and nine touchdowns. In 1962 he led the nation with a 43.4 punting average. He was a troubled player who actually was enrolled at Texas and TCU before going to a junior college. After an altercation with an assistant coach during the 1963 season, he was dismissed from the team and never returned.

Wayne Lee (Center, Linebacker) 1960–1962; All-America 1962: Lee was a top blocker and cocaptain of the Sooners' 1962

Big 8 championship team. He led the Sooners in tackles in home games in 1960.

Max Boydston (End) 1951–1954; All-America 1954: Boydston averaged 24.2 yards a catch during his career at OU. He took the ball away from the Oklahoma State quarterback in the 1953 game and ran 43 yards for a score in a 42–7 victory.

Buck McPhail (Fullback, Punter) 1950–1952; All-America 1952: In 1951 he averaged 8.56 yards a carry and in 1952 rushed for more than 1,000 yards during a season in which Billy Vessels won the Heisman Trophy. In 1952 he averaged 39.8 yards a punt.

Frankie Anderson (End) 1948–1950; All-America 1950: Anderson averaged 20.2 yards per catch and scored six touchdowns in his career at OU. In 1948 he tackled Iowa State backs for 50 yards in losses in a 33–6 OU victory.

George Thomas (Halfback, Defensive Back) 1946–1949; All-America 1949: Thomas rushed for 2,230 yards and 30 touchdowns during his OU career, breaking most of the Sooners' scoring records. He added six receiving touchdowns in his career. He was one of the best cover men in college football, either passing or running.

Paul "Buddy" Burris (Guard) 1946–1948; All-America all three seasons: Burris paved the way for Sooners' backs such as George Thomas to have big years. His line play helped get the Bud Wilkinson dynasty started at OU. He was the first of four Burris brothers from Muskogee, Oklahoma, to play at OU.

Plato Andros (Guard) 1941, 1946; All-America 1946: Andros started to play at OU before War World II, but served four years with the Coast Guard fighting against Nazi submarines. He returned to become an All-American at guard going both ways. His brother Dee was another Oklahoma lineman who later became the head football coach at Oregon State.

Pete Smith (Tackle) 1935–1937; All-America 1937: Smith was a great blocker on the Sooners' 1937 team, but he also was a lock-down defensive player who helped limit opponents to less than 40 yards passing per game in 1937. He was drafted in the third round in 1938 by the Detroit Lions.

J.W. "Dub" Wheeler (Tackle) 1933–1935; All-America 1935: Wheeler was part of an offensive line that allowed the Sooners to lead the conference in rushing in 1935. He was part of a defensive line that limited three teams under 70 yards rushing, also in 1935. He was the first Sooner to be selected in the pro football draft, in 1936, to Green Bay in the second round.

Cassius Gentry (Tackle/Punter) 1933–1934; All-America 1934: Gentry was the fastest player at OU during his career. He blocked three punts against Iowa State in 1933 in a 19–7 OU victory. He doubled as a punter for the Sooners, and after one punt he made the tackle on the play.

Roy "Soupy" Smoot (Tackle) 1918–1921; All-America 1920: Smoot became the first OU lineman to be named an All-American. In a 7–7 tie with Nebraska in 1919, Smoot blocked a punt before it left the punter's foot, and also did that against Missouri in a 6–6 tie the same year. Oklahoma won the Missouri Valley Conference in 1920, with Smoot as one of the stars.

Phil White (Halfback) 1918–1920; All-America 1920: A quadruple threat as a rusher-passer, defender, kicker, and returner, White played the 1920 season with a dislocated shoulder. He was the first halfback at OU to become an All-American.

92 Top OU Running Backs

DeMarco Murray, 2007–2010: As a sophomore in 2008, Murray rushed for 1,002 yards and 14 touchdowns after opening his career with five rushing touchdowns against North Texas in 2007. He finished with 3,685 career rushing yards on 759 attempts, the second-highest amount of career rushing attempts in OU history. His 50 career rushing touchdowns ranks third in the Sooner record book.

Quentin Griffin, 1999–2002: Griffin set a OU single-game touchdown record with six scores in a 63–14 rout of Texas in 2000. He led Oklahoma in rushing for three straight seasons, from 2000 through 2002, and notched 44 rushing touchdowns. He had another big day against Texas in 2002 with a career-high 248 rushing yards in a 35–24 OU victory.

De' Mond Parker, 1996–1998: His 291 yards rushing against Texas in 1997 is second on the OU charts behind Greg Pruitt's 294 yards against Kansas State in 1971. He had 16 100-yard rushing games in his OU career. He finished with 3,403 career rushing yards, despite leaving OU after three seasons for a brief NFL career.

Stanley Wilson, 1979–1982: No. 32 was a familiar blocker, the wishbone set-up man, but he still managed to lead the Sooners with 1,095 yards rushing as a junior in 1981. His 3,198 yards rushing in his OU career ranks among the Sooners' top 10 runners.

Jim Grisham, 1962–1964: Grisham was a consensus All-American in 1963 and three-time All–Big 8 selection. He rushed for 2,404 yards and 18 touchdowns during his career at OU. In Bud Wilkinson's final game in 1963 against Oklahoma State, he rallied the Sooners with four touchdowns in a 34–10 victory. His 218 yards rushing against the Cowboys was a Sooners rushing record at the time.

Clendon Thomas, 1955–1957: Thomas was a consensus All-American in 1957 and led the Sooners in scoring in both 1956 and 1957. In 1956 he accounted for 18 touchdowns, and in 1957 he finished ninth in the Heisman Trophy balloting. He rushed for 2,199 yards in his career and had 31 rushing touchdowns. The 6'2", 196-pounder had a 6.8 yards-per-carry career average. He

DeMarco Murray celebrates his 65-yard touchdown run against Texas on October 6, 2007, in Dallas.

was drafted in the second round by the Los Angeles Rams in 1958 and played four seasons for the Rams and seven for the Pittsburgh Steelers.

Leon Heath, 1948–1950: Heath had a career-high and then a Sooners record 170 yards rushing in OU's Sugar Bowl victory over Louisiana State. He was named the Most Outstanding Player of the January 2, 1950, Sugar Bowl. He averaged 9.5 yards a rush during the 1949 season. A consensus All-American during OU's first national title season of 1950, Heath was the fourth player taken in the 1951 draft by the Washington Redskins. He played for the Redskins for three seasons.

Honorable Mention: Jerald Moore, 1993–1995; Mike Gaddis, 1988–1991; Lydell Carr, 1984–1987; Spencer Tillman, 1983–1986; Marcus Dupree, 1982; David Overstreet, 1977–1980; Elvis Peacock, 1974–1977; Joe Wylie, 1970–1972; Leon Crosswhite, 1970–1972; Billy Pricer, 1954–1956; and Joe Golding, 1941, 1946.

(Please note: Billy Vessels, Billy Sims, Steve Owens, Joe Washington, Greg Pruitt, Tommy McDonald, Joe Don Looney, George Thomas, Spot Geyer, Claude Reeds, Buck McPhail, and Adrian Peterson are mentioned elsewhere.)

93 Top OU Quarterbacks

Josh Heupel, 1999–2000: Heupel was part of the Bob Stoops revival of the Sooners' football program with 7–5 and 13–0 records in the 1999 and 2000 seasons, respectively. He was the quarterback for OU's last national title team, which beat Florida State 13–2 in the Orange Bowl at the conclusion of the 2000 season. He was the first Sooner to have more than 1,000 passing attempts in a career (1,025), and he completed 63.8 percent of the passes for nearly 7,500 yards in just two seasons. Heupel has been the Sooners' quarterbacks coach since 2005. His most recent pupil is Heisman Trophy winner Sam Bradford.

Jamelle Holieway, 1985–1988: Holieway quarterbacked the Sooners to three Big 8 titles and one national title. He led the Sooners in passing in four straight seasons and in rushing two seasons during his career. He had 2,713 yards rushing and 2,430 yards passing. Holieway took over for an injured Troy Aikman as a freshman and became the Sooners' star.

J.C. Watts, 1978–1980: Watts was the Most Outstanding Offensive Player in back-to-back Orange Bowl victories in the 1979 and 1980 seasons. During his career he was 22–3 in 25 starts. Watts was the total offense leader for the Sooners in their wishbone offense in 1980. Later he became a United States Congressman from the Fourth District in Oklahoma. He was born in Eufaula, Oklahoma, home of the Selmon brothers.

Thomas Lott, 1976–1978: Lott compiled a 23–5–1 record as the Sooners' starting quarterback. The San Antonio, Texas, native was All-Conference as a junior and senior. He was always a big threat to run—he scored twice in a 31–24 victory over Nebraska in the January 1, 1979, Orange Bowl.

Steve Davis, 1973–1975: A three-year starter, Davis had a 32–1–1 record and was a part of three Big 8 titles and two national titles. His 32 victories by a quarterback ranks No. 1 in OU history. Davis was the Orange Bowl's Offensive MVP in his final game, a 14–6 victory over Michigan, which clinched the 1975 national title. Davis rushed for 2,124 yards and passed for 2,036 yards as a dual threat.

Jack Mildren, 1969–1971: The original wishbone key turner, he rushed for 1,289 yards in 1971 when Oklahoma set the NCAA

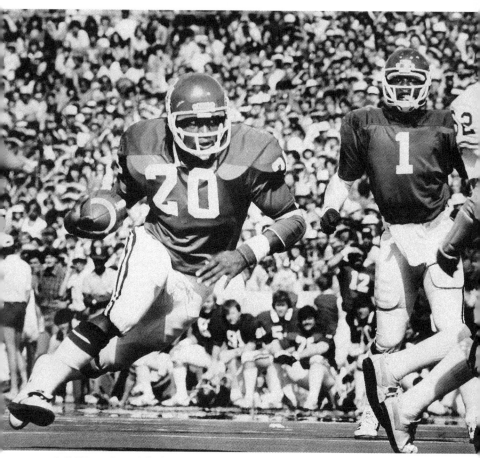

J.C. Watts (No. 1) looks on after handing the ball off to Billy Sims during the Sooners' 38–9 victory over Iowa State in October 1979.

rushing season record. He ran for two scores and passed for two in the 35–31 Game of the Century loss to Nebraska. He accounted for 32 rushing touchdowns and 24 passing touchdowns during his career. The 1971 All-American was drafted in the second round by the Baltimore Colts and played three years in the NFL. From 1990 to 1994, he was Lieutenant Governor of Oklahoma.

Jimmy Harris, 1954–1956: Harris was 31–0 as the Sooners' starting quarterback in the middle of the 47-game OU winning streak. As a senior, he passed for eight touchdowns and completed 62.2 percent of his passes. He played briefly in the NFL, but came back and got his geology degree, and he assisted Bud Wilkinson in 1959.

Claude Arnold, 1948–1950: Arnold led the Sooners to their first national title in 1950. He passed for 1,069 yards in 1950, with 13 touchdowns and one interception. Arnold, All–Big 7 as a senior, rushed for 134 yards and two touchdowns in a 27–18 victory over Colorado in 1950, when most of the other offensive stars were out with injuries.

Jack Mitchell, 1946–1948: Mitchell was the first Oklahoma quarterback to win All-America honors (1948). He finished his Oklahoma career as the MVP of the 1949 Sugar Bowl, when the Sooners beat North Carolina 14–6. He scored the first touchdown of the game on a run. He went on to become a head football coach at Wichita State, Arkansas, and Kansas.

Honorable Mention: Cale Gundy, 1990–1993; Danny Bradley, 1981–1984; Bob Warmack, 1966–1968; and Darrell Royal, 1946–1949.

(Please note: Landry Jones, Jason White, Sam Bradford, Eddie Crowder, Jack Jacobs, and Darrell Royal are mentioned elsewhere.)

94 Bedlam in 2013

Oklahoma's 33–24 victory over the instate rival Cowboys in the 2013 regular-season final was improbable on the surface, but completely in keeping with the history of this series. The poor Cowboys over the years often have not been able to close a game against the Sooners when it means the most.

And this was a classic example of that trend. Had the Cowboys defended their home field in Stillwater the way many expected they would, they would have had a share of the Big 12 Conference title and a trip to the final BCS with a berth in the Fiesta Bowl.

Instead, the bitter loss to the Sooners sent Baylor to the Fiesta Bowl as the undisputed Big 12 champions and relegated the Cowboys to the Cotton Bowl and a second-place Big 12 tie with OU. Oklahoma was awarded a berth in the BCS' Sugar Bowl. And what looked just like an average finish for OU turned into a very good one when the Sooners upset Alabama 45–31 in New Orleans.

Against OSU, the Sooners had to use three different quarterbacks in the game, some trickery. a hot field-goal kicker, and a couple of comebacks to pull out the victory. They scored touchdowns on offense, defense, and special teams (two) before a hostile crowd.

OU starting quarterback Trevor Knight suffered a shoulder injury to his non-throwing shoulder in the second quarter of a game that ended up a 10–10 tie at halftime. Knight did not return and was replaced by Blake Bell and third-string quarterback Kendal Thompson, son of former Sooner Charles Thompson. Thompson started at the beginning of the second half because he was better at the zone read and option according to OU coach Bob Stoops.

"But they were just bringing everybody in the box, and we knew we had to get out of that," Stoops said. "Blake Bell went in and did a great job. I am really proud of his poise. He scrambled around and made some plays on his own."

A key play in the game occurred in the third quarter with the Sooners trailing 17–10. The Sooners lined up for a field-goal try by reliable kicker Michael Hunnicutt, who set an OU record for field goals in a season. Instead, Stoops had holder Grant Bothun keep the ball and throw an eight-yard scoring strike to Hunnicutt. Instead of trailing 17–13 after making a potential field goal, the Sooners had tied the score at 17–17.

"I felt at that point, here we are on our third quarterback and I just thought a field goal wasn't going to be good enough," Stoops said. "I knew we were going to need more than that. We had a numbers advantage out to that side, the way they were lining up. And it worked out."

Hunnicutt kicked a go-ahead field goal to put OU up 20–17, but OSU answered with a touchdown with 1:46 remaining when the Cowboys scored on a one-yard run for a 24–20 lead.

Blake countered with a seven-yard pass to Jalen Saunders with 19 seconds remaining in the game, Bell was 5-for-8 for 57 yards on the 66-yard winning drive as OU rallied again.

"I was even licking my chops because I was ready for that one," Bell said of the game-winning touchdown pass. "Once we got the play call and Jalen ran a great route on that play, I just put it out there to him and he went and got it. It's a tough one. You're down there and scrunched down in a tight zone and you only have so much room to throw it [into]. He did a great job of getting the guy off him, and I just threw it out there for him."

Oklahoma coach Bob Stoops beat OSU coach Mike Gundy for the eighth time in nine tries when OU scored an insurance touchdown on a fumble recovery in the end zone in the closing seconds.

95 Top OU Linebackers

Curtis Lofton, 2005–2007, was the 2007 Big 12 Defensive Player of Year. He started only in 2007, but made 156 total tackles (unassisted and assisted) and 10.5 tackles for losses. He was the second-round selection of the Atlanta Falcons in the 2008 NFL Draft and was a 2007 consensus All-America player.

Rufus Alexander, 2003–2006, led OU in tackles in back-to-back seasons as a junior and a senior; was an All-American in 2006 as a senior, when he had 118 tackles (75 unassisted); started 36 games in his career, including the entire 2005 and 2006 seasons; and was the 2006 Big 12 Defensive Player of Year.

Teddy Lehman, 2000–2003, won the Bednarik (best defensive player in the county) and Butkus (best linebacker) Awards as a senior; was All-America in 2002 and 2003; had 117 tackles as a senior, 19-for-47 yards in losses; and caught an interception for a touchdown from the 1-yard line, sealing a 14–3 victory over Texas in 2001.

Rocky Calmus, 1998–2001, won the Butkus Award (best linebacker in the country) in 2001, was All-America in 2000 and 2001, had 117 tackles (72 unassisted) as a senior, and ranks fourth in career tackles at OU.

Joe Bowden, 1989–1991, was Big 8 Defensive Newcomer of the Year as a sophomore in 1989, in 1991 was an All-America player, had two interceptions he returned for touchdowns his senior season, and was drafted by the Houston Oilers and played in NFL from 1992 to 2000.

Brian Bosworth, 1984–1986, was the only back-to-back winner of Butkus Award (best linebacker in the country) in 1985 and 1986, was nicknamed "the Boz" for his flamboyant play and mouthy interviews, was a consensus All-American in 1985 and 1986, and was OU's top tackler in each season of his college career and an Academic All-American as a senior.

Dante Jones, 1984–1987, was a consensus All-American in 1987 as a senior. As a junior, he was the Most Outstanding Defensive Player in OU's Orange Bowl victory against Arkansas, and as a senior led OU in total tackles with 118. He played eight seasons in the NFL first with Chicago, then Denver.

Jackie Shipp, 1980–1983, was All–Big 8 in 1982 and 1983 and had the Sooners' record 23 tackles against Missouri in 1981. As a sophomore, he had 189 tackles, which ranks first in a season at OU and was second in career tackles at OU.

Rod Shoate, 1972–1974, was only OU's second three-time All-American, recorded 21 tackles against Texas in 1974 in a 16–13 victory, and ranks fifth in career tackles at OU. He played for the New England Patriots for seven seasons.

Curtis Lofton returns an interception 26 yards in the Big 12 Conference championship game against Missouri in San Antonio in December 2007.

George Cumby, 1976–1979, was an All-American in 1977 and 1979 (consensus), was named Big 8 Defensive Player of the Year twice, and ranks third in career tackles category at OU. He was the first-round draft pick by Green Bay, where he played six seasons.

Daryl Hunt, 1975–1978, was an All-American in 1977 and 1978 and the career leader in tackles at OU. He led the Sooners in tackles each season from 1976 to 1978 and had seven career interceptions.

Carl McAdams, 1963–1965, was an All-American in 1964 and 1965 (consensus). Head coach Gomer Jones said McAdams was so quick, "He could take two steps the wrong way…and still recover in time to make the play." McAdams led OU with five interceptions in 1964 and was drafted in the third round by the New York Jets in 1966, where he played three seasons.

(Please note: Jerry Tubbs and Kurt Burris are mentioned elsewhere.)

96 Top OU Receivers

Ryan Broyles, 2008–11, was the most productive receiver in Sooner history. When the two-time All-American left, he owned eight of the nine major school records for receiving. His junior season he led major-college football with 9.36 receptions a game. His senior season he became major-college football's all-time career receptions leader and had 4,586 career receiving yards and 45 touchdowns at OU. Selected by Detroit Lions in second round of the 2012 draft.

Kenny Stills, 2010–12, played somewhat in the shadows of Broyles but still ranks fourth in career touchdown receptions at OU (24) and fourth in receiving yards during his career (2,594).

He had 204 receptions in just three seasons before he left after his junior year and was drafted in the fifth round by the New Orleans Saints.

Juaquin Iglesias, 2005–2008, a Kileen, Texas, native, had 74 catches for 1,150 yards and 10 touchdowns as a senior in 2008. He caught the then OU-record 12 passes for 191 yards in a 2008 victory over Kansas. He still ranks third in career receiving yards at OU (2,861) behind Broyles and Mark Clayton and fourth in OU career receptions (202).

Malcolm Kelly, 2005–2007, averaged a team-best 16.8 yards per catch in 2007. His other numbers: 49 receptions, 821 yards, and nine touchdowns. As a sophomore, he had 62 catches for 993 yards and 10 touchdowns. Through the 2013 season, his 21 career touchdown catches ranked No. 5 at OU. He left after his junior season and was selected by the Washington Redskins in the second round of the 2008 NFL Draft, but injuries kept his pro career from ever really materializing.

Jermaine Gresham, 2006–08, caught two touchdown passes, OU's only scores in a 24–14 loss to Florida in the BCS title game at the Orange Bowl on January 8, 2009. The Ardmore, Oklahoma, native had 26 career touchdown receptions (which ranks third at OU) and a career-best 14 touchdown receptions in 2008 (that is still tied for third at OU in a single season). Despite missing most of his senior season with a knee injury, Gresham was drafted in the first round by the Cincinnati Bengals in the 2010 draft and since has been named to two Pro Bowls.

Mark Clayton, 2001–2004, is a two-time All-American. He had a career-high 190 yards receiving in a 65–13 victory over Texas in 2003 and ranks second at OU in receiving yards for a career (3,241) and second in career touchdown receptions (31). As an Oklahoma receiver Clayton had 533 yards receiving after he caught the ball. He was selected in the first round of the 2005 NFL Draft by the Baltimore Ravens and later played for the St. Louis Rams.

Tinker Owens, 1972–1975, was an All-American from Miami, Oklahoma, and was the brother of OU Heisman Trophy winner Steve Owens. He was MVP of the 1972 Sugar Bowl during the 14–0 victory over Penn State, with five catches for 132 yards and a touchdown. He averaged 22.9 yards a catch during his OU career and played five seasons for the New Orleans Saints.

Steve Zabel, 1967–1969, caught 64 passes for 885 yards and eight touchdowns in his career, but averaged 13.8 yards a catch. He was a sophomore in 1967, when he caught the game-winning touchdown pass against Kansas to secure an Orange Bowl berth. He was taken sixth overall in the 1970 draft by the Philadelphia Eagles and played 10 seasons in the NFL with three different teams.

Eddie Hinton, 1966–1968, was All–Big 8 as a senior. The Lawton, Oklahoma, native led the Sooners in receiving in 1967 and 1968. Hinton's 123 career receptions stood as an OU record for 34 years. He was selected by the Baltimore Colts in the first round of the 1969 NFL Draft and later played in the Colts' victory over the Dallas Cowboys in Super Bowl V.

Honorable Mention: Antwone Savage, 1999–2002; Stephen Alexander, 1994–1997; Billy Brooks, 1973–1975; Corey Warren, 1990–1993; Trent Smith, 1999–2002; Travis Wilson, 2002–2005; and Curtis Fagan, 1999–2002.

(Please note Keith Jackson is mentioned elsewhere.)

97 Top OU Defensive Backs

Roy Williams, 1999–2001, won the Jim Thorpe Award (best defensive back in the nation) and the Nagurski Award (best defensive player in the nation) in 2001. He made 34 tackles for 134

Mark Clayton grabs a touchdown pass in front of University of Colorado's Phil Jackson in November 2002.

yards in losses during his three-year career, and in 2001 was seventh in the Heisman Trophy voting after intercepting five passes and making 14 tackles for 57 yards in losses. He was selected in the first round (eighth overall) by the Dallas Cowboys in the 2002 NFL Draft after bypassing his senior season.

Derrick Strait, 2000–2003, won the Jim Thorpe Award and Nagurski Award in 2003, two seasons after Roy Williams made the same sweep of the two awards. He made 14 interceptions in his career and returned them for a school record 397 yards, and set a school record for career starts (53). The Austin, Texas, native was a one-man wrecking crew against Texas in 2003 (a 65–13 OU victory) with 11 tackles, an interception, two fumble recoveries, and three pass deflections.

Quinton Carter, 2006, 2008–10, native of Las Vegas, was only a two-year starter for the Sooners. But he is just one of two Sooner defensive backs to register 88 tackles or more in a season and the only one to do it in back-to-back seasons (2009–10). He was selected in the fourth round of the NFL draft by the Denver Broncos.

Rickey Dixon, 1984–1987, was the first OU winner of the Thorpe Award and had 17 career interceptions, including a Sooners record nine in a season as a senior. His fourth-quarter interception against Nebraska in 1987 sealed OU's 17–7 victory and an Orange Bowl berth. He was the fifth player taken overall in the 1988 NFL Draft by Cincinnati and played six total seasons in the NFL, first with the Bengals and then with the Los Angeles Raiders.

Darrol Ray, 1976–1979, was All–Big 8 in 1978 and 1979, had a career-high eight interceptions in 1978, and had 302 yards in returns during his career at OU, ranking third. He was drafted by the New York Jets in the second round of the 1980 NFL Draft and played for five seasons there.

Zac Henderson, 1974–1977, was named the nation's outstanding defensive back at the Heisman Trophy ceremony in 1977. A four-year starter, he had 299 career tackles. In 1977 he had seven interceptions and 15 total for his career and made All-America in 1976 and in 1977 (consensus).

Randy Hughes, 1972–1974, made All-America in 1974 and All–Big 8 in 1973 and '74. He had 14 career interceptions and returned two for touchdowns and broke up 23 passes in his career, including 12 as a senior. The Academic All-American was drafted in the fourth round of the 1975 NFL Draft by Dallas and played six seasons for the Cowboys.

Brandon Everage, 2000–2003, played four seasons for the Sooners and made All-America in 2002, when he had six interceptions and 107 yards in returns. In his career, he had 10 interceptions, 14 tackles for loss, and 28 passes broken up. He played at times more like a linebacker because he had 285 career tackles.

Buddy Jones, 1947–1950, although only 5'10", 155 pounds played bigger than his size and made All-America in 1950. In 1949 Jones was a big reason the Sooners gave up only five touchdown passes in an unbeaten season. He was a standout in OU's two Sugar Bowl wins during the 1948 and 1949 seasons.

(Please note: Darrell Royal, Eddie Crowder, J.T. Thatcher, and George Thomas are listed elsewhere.)

98 Top OU Defensive Linemen

Gerald McCoy, 2007–09, collected All-America honors during both the 2008 and 2009 seasons and became the Sooners' 35th two-time All-American at the time. Over the course of his career he posted 33 tackles for 141 yards in losses, including 14.5 sacks.

Dan Cody, 2000–2004, made All-America as a senior in 2004 and was injured early in the 2001 season and given an extra year of eligibility. In his career he had 25 sacks for 162 yards in losses.

Tommie Harris, 2001–2003, won the Lombardi Trophy in 2003 and was a finalist for the Nagurski Trophy the same season. He was a two-time All-American, and in 2003, as a junior, had 10 tackles for losses (39 yards) and 19 quarterback hurries. He was selected by the Chicago Bears 14th overall in the 2004 NFL Draft after opting to leave college football a year early for the pros.

Tony Casillas, 1982–1985, was a two-time All-American and won the Lombardi Award in 1985. In his four-year career, he had 40 tackles for loss (248 yards). He was the second player taken overall in the 1986 NFL Draft by the Atlanta Falcons and played in Atlanta, with the New York Jets, and with the Dallas Cowboys.

Tommie Harris closes in on Baylor quarterback Shawn Bell in a November 2003 game in Norman.

Kelly Gregg, 1995–1998, was All–Big 12 in 1997 and 1998 during the John Blake era and ranks second at OU in career tackles for loss with 53. He has had a successful career with the Baltimore Ravens and was part of the team that beat the New York Giants in Super Bowl XXXV.

Cedric Jones, 1992–1995, made five sacks, an OU record, in a 1994 victory over Texas Tech. He set an OU record with 14 sacks in 1995 and is the OU career leader in sacks with 31.5. He was selected No. 5 overall in the 1996 NFL Draft by the New York Giants and played five seasons there.

Darrell Reed, 1984–1987, was an All-American in 1987, when OU defense limited teams to eight points a game. He was one of only three Sooners to be selected All-Conference four times and had 40 tackles for losses (187 yards) in his career.

Kevin Murphy, 1981–1985, of Richardson, Texas, was All-America in 1985 and All–Big 8 three times, 1982, 1983, and 1985. He had 21 tackles in a 1983 loss to Missouri. His best season was in 1983, when he had 144 total tackles and 13 tackles for 84 yards in losses.

Rick Bryan, 1980–1983, a Coweta, Oklahoma, native, was All-America in 1982 and 1983, and All–Big 8 from 1981 to 1983. He had 365 tackles in his career at OU, which is among OU's top 10. He was selected in the first round of the 1984 NFL Draft by Atlanta and played a decade with the Falcons.

Reggie Kinlaw, 1975–1978, a Miami, Florida, native, was All-America in 1977 and 1978. In 1978 he had 120 total tackles and seven tackles for loss (27 yards). He was selected in the 12th round of the 1979 NFL Draft by Oakland and played six seasons with the franchise.

Jimbo Elrod, 1973–1975, was All-America in 1975 and had 44 tackles for loss in his career at OU. In 1974, against Texas, he caused Earl Campbell to fumble, setting up OU in field position to kick the winning field goal in a 16–13 victory. He was selected in the fifth round by Kansas City in the 1976 NFL Draft and played three seasons there and one in Houston.

Derland Moore, 1970–1972, was All-America in 1972. In just three seasons, he had 223 tackles from his tackle spot and was drafted in the second round by the New Orleans Saints in 1973. He spent most of his 14-year career with the Saints.

Granville Liggins, 1965–1967, weighed only 214 pounds. The Tulsa, Oklahoma, native was UPI Lineman of the Year in 1967 and usually had to beat bigger linemen with his quickness, of which UT coach Darrell Royal said, "He moves so fast he looks like he is offsides." He was All-America in 1966 and 1967 (consensus).

Granville Norris, 1925–1927, a Laverne, Oklahoma, native was named All-America in 1927. He had the most blocked punts in the Missouri Valley Conference in 1926. In 1927 he dominated Kansas' offense in a 26–7 OU victory.

Gilford Duggan, 1937–1939, was a part of OU's 1938 defense that allowed only 43.3 yards a game. In 1937 he was a part of a defense that posted five shutouts. Drafted in the 15th round by the New York Giants in 1940, he played with five different professional teams.

Frank "Pop" Ivy, 1937–1939, made All-America in 1939. Sports writer Grantland Rice called Ivy one of the greatest defensive ends he had ever seen. In 1938 the OU defense allowed only two touchdowns during the regular season.

(Please note: Lee Roy, Lucious, and Dewey Selmon, were all All-America defensive linemen and are mentioned elsewhere.)

99 Top OU Offensive Linemen

Duke Robinson, 2005–2008, was a 2008 Outland Trophy Finalist and was a two-time All-American, in 2007 and 2008. He played offensive tackle in high school and switched positions.

Anthony Phillips, 1985–1988, made All-America in 1986 and 1988 (consensus) and was All–Big 8 all four seasons. He was a four-time All-Academic selection in the Big 8.

Mark Hutson, 1984–1987, was a two-time All-American in 1986 and 1987 (consensus) and was All–Big 8 three times. A rare starter as a freshman, then–assistant coach Merv Johnson said of Hutson that he was "one of the most fundamentally solid and sound linemen I have ever worked with."

Greg Roberts, 1975–1978, was an Outland Trophy winner in 1978 as the nation's top interior lineman, and was All-America in 1977 and 1978 (consensus). In his senior season, most of the plays were run over his right guard spot for Heisman Trophy winner Billy Sims. OU led the nation in scoring and rushing in 1978 and was second in total offense.

Tom Brahaney, 1970–1972, was a big blocker on the top rushing team in college football history in 1971. He was a finalist for the Lombardi Trophy in 1972, a consensus All-American in 1971 and 1972, and was inducted into the College Football Hall of Fame in 2007.

Bill Krisher, 1955–1957, was a two-time All-American in 1956 and in 1957 (consensus). He opened up holes for All-America running back Clendon Thomas and was drafted in the third round by the Pittsburgh Steelers in 1958 and played there before going to Dallas in the American Football League.

Bill Bolinger, 1953–1955, was one of the famous "B Boys" from Muskogee, Oklahoma, and was a consensus All-American in 1955. In 1955 Bolinger finished ninth in the Heisman Trophy balloting. He was credited with blocking for an offense that finished No. 1 in the country in rushing and total offensive yards per game for the unbeaten and national champion Sooners.

Tom Catlin, 1950–1952, a two-time All-American in 1951 and 1952, was cocaptain of the 1952 Oklahoma team that was 8–1–1. An outstanding student, he was OU's first Academic All-American. He later played in the NFL for five years with the Cleveland Browns and Philadelphia Eagles. He also served in the Air Force during the Korean War and was an assistant for Red Blaik at Army.

Stanley West, 1946–1949, was an All-American in 1949 when he was cocaptain of an unbeaten team (11–0). He sprang holes for three different OU conference rushing champions during his OU days. He was the 12th player taken overall in the 1950 draft by the Los Angeles Rams and played eight seasons in the NFL.

Wade Walker, 1946–1949, was one of only three OU players to receive all-conference honors during four seasons. He was a big blocker for three excellent OU backs: Joe Golding, George Brewer, and George Thomas. Walker later was head football coach at Mississippi State and then Oklahoma's athletics director.

Honorable Mention: Gabe Ikard, 2010–13; Trent Williams, 2006–09; Vince Carter, 2001–2004; Terry Crouch, 1979–1981; Louis Oubre, 1978–1980; Mike Vaughan, 1974–1976; Terry Webb, 1973–1975; John Roush, 1972–1974; Kyle Davis, 1972–1974; Eddie Foster, 1971–1973; Ken Mendenhall, 1967–1969; Leon Cross, 1960–1962; Jerry Thompson, 1957–1959; Bob Harrison, 1956–1958; and Ed Gray, 1954–1956.

(Please note: Outland Trophy winners Jammal Brown, Jim Weatherall, and J.D. Roberts are mentioned elsewhere.)

100 Sweet Sugar Bowl Redemption

Oklahoma coach Bob Stoops has let his thoughts be well known about the relative strength of the Southeastern Conference to other leagues before the 2013 season. The SEC had won seven straight national championships before the Atlantic Coast Conference's Florida State beat Auburn for the 2013 crown.

Stoops, which had called the SEC's touting of itself as the strongest conference "propaganda", got to savor the 45–31 upset of SEC powerhouse Alabama in the Sugar Bowl on January 2, 2014. His Sooners dominated the team that had won the last two national titles in 2011 and 2012

Stoops has disagreed that the SEC is the best conference in college football, pointing out that the teams at the bottom of the league are not competitive with the powerhouse programs. In other words, the Big 12 Conference, of which Oklahoma is a member, might have better depth.

"I am not going to expound on that," Stoops said after the Sugar Bowl. "I won't have to dodge any punches, I guess you could say that. ...So enough of that....I admire the way they [Alabama] play, I really do, and Coach Saban and the way they do things. I'm not pointing any fingers, but I think sometimes the comparisons aren't necessarily very true."

The Sooners' victory over the Crimson Tide was a strong antidote to any hangover from their lopsided 41–13 loss to another SEC team, Texas A&M, in the Cotton Bowl after the 2012 season. Aggie quarterback Johnny Manziel accounted for 516 yards and four touchdowns in that game. Florida also beat Oklahoma, 24–14, in the BCS title game after the 2008 season.

But Stoops downplayed any lack of confidence against SEC teams, claiming "we weren't coming in here [to the Sugar Bowl] on a pile of wood." He added, "We have a lot of confidence in what we do, too."

Oklahoma's freshman redshirt quarterback Trevor Knight set a Sugar Bowl record for pass completions (32), amassing 348 yards and four touchdowns.

"Trevor Knight, of course, was exceptional," Stoops said. "I think he showed the whole country what we have been watching for two years in our practices and scrimmages and things like that, that the game has started to slow down for him where he's really starting to feel comfortable in what he can do. He's got a very live arm, with great legs."

Oklahoma center Gabe Ikard said before the game beating two-time defending national champion Alabama was important for the perception of Oklahoma football. The Sooners suffered consecutive BCS losses to LSU, USC, Boise State, West Virginia, and Florida from 2003 to 2008 before beating UConn in the Fiesta Bowl on January 1, 2011.

"It shows you that we're still one of the premier, top-five programs in the country," Ikard said. "We win 10 games every year and people still feel we've fallen off, so it will be big for recruiting, big for the programs, and big for the fan base."

Sources

Barry Switzer, www.switzertalentagency.com.

Billy Sims Barbecue Restaurants, billysimsbbq.com.

Daily Oklahoman, 1957–2008.

Dallas Morning News (1987–2008).

Dean Blevins bio on News9.com.

Duffey, Gene and Steve Richardson. *60 Years of the Outland Trophy*. Dallas: Attriad Press, 2006.

ESPN.com.

Fed Ex Orange Bowl Media Guide, 2005.

Fed Ex Orange Bowl Media Guide, 2009.

Internet Movie Database, imdb.com.

Lee Roy Selmon Restaurants website, leeroyselmons.com.

McCallum, John D. *Big Eight Football*. New York: Charles Scribner's Sons, 1979.

Museum of the Gulf Coast website, museumofthegulfcoast.org.

National Football Foundation website, footballfoundation.com.

Native American Magazine, 1999.

O'Connell's Restaurant website, oconnellsnorman.com.

Official 2008 Division I-A and I-AA Football Records Book, Indianapolis, Indiana: The National Collegiate Athletic Association, 2008.

Oklahoma Sports Hall of Fame/Jim Thorpe web site, jimthorpeassoc.com.

Oregon State University Media Guide, 2008.

Oregonian, September 24, 2008.

Othello's website, othellosnorman.com.

Smith, Loran. *Fifty Years on the Fifty: The Orange Bowl Story*. Charlotte, North Carolina: Fast & McMillan Publishers, 1983.

Sooner Legends Inn website, soonerlegends.com.

Southeastern Conference Football Media Guide, 2004.

State Fair of Texas website, bigtex.com.

Ted Watts website, tedwatts.org.

University of Georgia Football Media Guide, 2007.

University of Kansas Football Media Guide, 2008.

University of Notre Dame Football Media Guide, 2003.

University of Oklahoma web site, ou.edu.

University of Oklahoma Sports Information website, soonersports. com.

University of Oklahoma Football Media Guide, 2004, 2008.

University of Oklahoma Department of Athletics, Annual Report, 2007–2008.

University of Texas Spring Football Media Guide, 2006.

University of South Carolina Football Media Guide, 2008.

University of Washington Football Media Guide, 2008.

Washington State University website, wsucougars.cstv.com.